ANATOMY OF THE
WORKS MINIS

Other Veloce publications -

Great Cars
Austin-Healey – A celebration of the fabulous 'Big' Healey (Piggott)
Jaguar E-type (Thorley)
Jaguar Mark 1 & 2 (Thorley)
Triumph TR – TR2 to 6: The last of the traditional sports cars (Piggott)

Rally Giants Series
Audi Quattro (Robson)
Austin Healey 100-6 & 3000 (Robson)
Fiat 131 Abarth (Robson)
Ford Escort MkI (Robson)
Ford Escort RS Cosworth & World Rally Car (Robson)
Ford Escort RS1800 (Robson)
Lancia Delta 4WD/Integrale (Robson)
Lancia Stratos (Robson)
Mini Cooper/Mini Cooper S (Robson)
Peugeot 205 T16 (Robson)
Saab 96 & V4 (Robson)
Subaru Impreza (Robson)
Toyota Celica GT4 (Robson)

General
1½-litre GP Racing 1961-1965 (Whitelock)
AC Two-litre Saloons & Buckland Sportscars (Archibald)
Alfa Romeo 155/156/147 Competition Touring Cars (Collins)
Alfa Romeo Giulia Coupé GT & GTA (Tipler)
Alfa Romeo Montreal – The dream car that came true (Taylor)
Alfa Romeo Montreal – The Essential Companion (Classic Reprint of 500 copies) (Taylor)
Alfa Tipo 33 (McDonough & Collins)
Alpine & Renault – The Development of the Revolutionary Turbo F1 Car 1968 to 1979 (Smith)
Alpine & Renault – The Sports Prototypes 1963 to 1969 (Smith)
Alpine & Renault – The Sports Prototypes 1973 to 1978 (Smith)
An Austin Anthology (Stringer)
An Incredible Journey (Falls & Reisch)
Anatomy of the Classic Mini (Huthert & Ely)
Anatomy of the Works Minis (Moylan)
Armstrong-Siddeley (Smith)
Art Deco and British Car Design (Down)
Austin Cars 1948 to 1990 – a pictorial history (Rowe)
Autodrome (Collins & Ireland)
Automotive A-Z, Lane's Dictionary of Automotive Terms (Lane)
Automotive Mascots (Kay & Springate)
Bahamas Speed Weeks, The (O'Neil)
Bentley Continental, Corniche and Azure (Bennett)
Bentley MkVI, Rolls-Royce Silver Wraith, Dawn & Cloud/Bentley R & S-Series (Nutland)
Bluebird CN7 (Stevens)
BMC Competitions Department Secrets (Turner, Chambers & Browning)
BMW 5-Series (Cranswick)
BMW Z-Cars (Taylor)
BMW Boxer Twins 1970-1995 Bible, The (Falloon)
BMW Cafe Racers (Cloesen)
BMW Classic 5 Series 1972 to 2003 (Cranswick)
BMW Custom Motorcycles – Choppers, Cruisers, Bobbers, Trikes & Quads (Cloesen)
BMW – The Power of M (Vivian)
Bonjour – Is this Italy? (Turner)
British 250cc Racing Motorcycles (Pereira)
British at Indianapolis, The (Wagstaff)
British Café Racers (Cloesen)
British Cars, The Complete Catalogue of, 1895-1975 (Culshaw & Horrobin)
British Custom Motorcycles – The Brit Chop – choppers, cruisers, bobbers & trikes (Cloesen)
BRM – A Mechanic's Tale (Salmon)
BRM V16 (Ludvigsen)
BSA Bantam Bible, The (Henshaw)
BSA Motorcycles – the final evolution (Jones)
Bugatti – The eight-cylinder Touring Cars 1920-34 (Price & Arbey)
Bugatti Type 40 (Price)
Bugatti 46/50 Updated Edition (Price & Arbey)
Bugatti T44 & T49 (Price & Arbey)
Bugatti 57 2nd Edition (Price)
Bugatti Type 57 Grand Prix – A Celebration (Tomlinson)
Caravan, Improve & Modify Your (Porter)
Caravans, The Illustrated History 1919-1959 (Jenkinson)
Caravans, The Illustrated History From 1960 (Jenkinson)
Carrera Panamericana, La (Tipler)
Car-tastrophes – 80 automotive atrocities from the past 20 years (Honest John, Fowler)
Chrysler 300 – America's Most Powerful Car 2nd Edition (Ackerson)
Chrysler PT Cruiser (Ackerson)
Citroën DS (Bobbitt)
Classic British Car Electrical Systems (Astley)
Cobra – The Real Thing! (Legate)
Competition Car Aerodynamics 3rd Edition (McBeath)
Competition Car Composites A Practical Handbook (Revised 2nd Edition) (McBeath)
Concept Cars, How to illustrate and design – New 2nd Edition (Dewey)
Cortina – Ford's Bestseller (Robson)
Cosworth – The Search for Power (6th edition) (Robson)
Coventry Climax Racing Engines (Hammill)
Daily Mirror 1970 World Cup Rally 40, The (Robson)
Daimler SP250 New Edition (Long)
Datsun Fairlady Roadster to 280ZX – The Z-Car Story (Long)
Dino – The V6 Ferrari (Long)
Dodge Challenger & Plymouth Barracuda (Grist)
Dodge Charger – Enduring Thunder (Ackerson)
Dodge Dynamite! (Grist)
Dorset from the Sea – The Jurassic Coast from Lyme Regis to Old Harry Rocks photographed from its best viewpoint (also Souvenir Edition) (Belasco)
Draw & Paint Cars – How to (Gardiner)
Drive on the Wild Side, A – 20 Extreme Driving Adventures From Around the World (Weaver)
Ducati 750 Bible, The (Falloon)
Ducati 750 SS 'round-case' 1974, The Book of the (Falloon)
Ducati 860, 900 and Mille Bible, The (Falloon)
Ducati Monster Bible (New Updated & Revised Edition), The (Falloon)
Ducati Story, The - 6th Edition (Falloon)
Ducati 916 (updated edition) (Falloon)
Dune Buggy, Building A – The Essential Manual (Shakespeare)
Dune Buggy Files (Hale)
Dune Buggy Handbook (Hale)
East German Motor Vehicles in Pictures (Suhr/Weinreich)
Fast Ladies – Female Racing Drivers 1888 to 1970 (Bouzanquet)
Fate of the Sleeping Beauties, The (op de Weegh/Hottendorff/op de Weegh)
Ferrari 288 GTO, The Book of the (Sackey)
Ferrari 333 SP (O'Neil)
Fiat & Abarth 124 Spider & Coupé (Tipler)
Fiat & Abarth 500 & 600 - 2nd Edition (Bobbitt)
Fiats, Great Small (Ward)
Fine Art of the Motorcycle Engine, The (Peirce)
Ford Cleveland 335-Series V8 engine 1970 to 1982 – The Essential Source Book (Hammill)
Ford F100/F150 Pick-up 1948-1996 (Ackerson)
Ford F150 Pick-up 1997-2005 (Ackerson)
Ford Focus WRC (Robson)
Ford GT – Then, and Now (Streather)
Ford GT40 (Legate)
Ford Midsize Muscle - Fairlane, Torino & Ranchero (Cranswick)
Ford Model Y (Roberts)
Ford Small Block V8 Racing Engines 1962-1970 – The Essential Source Book (Hammill)
Ford Thunderbird From 1954, The Book of the (Long)
Formula One - The Real Score? (Harvey)
Formula 5000 Motor Racing, Back then ... and back now (Lawson)
Forza Minardi! (Vigar)
France: the essential guide for car enthusiasts – 200 things for the car enthusiast to see and do (Parish)
Franklin's Indians (Sucher/Pickering/Diamond/Havelin)
From Crystal Palace to Red Square – A Hapless Biker's Road to Russia (Turner)
Funky Mopeds (Skelton)
The Good, the Mad and the Ugly ... not to mention Jeremy Clarkson (Dron)
Grand Prix Ferrari – The Years of Enzo Ferrari's Power, 1948-1980 (Pritchard)
Grand Prix Ford – DFV-powered Formula 1 Cars (Robson)
GT – The World's Best GT Cars 1953-73 (Dawson)
Hillclimbing & Sprinting – The Essential Manual (Short & Wilkinson)
Honda NSX (Long)
How to Restore & Improve Classic Car Suspension, Steering & Wheels (Parish, translator)
Immortal Austin Seven (Morgan)
Inside the Rolls-Royce & Bentley Styling Department – 1971 to 2001 (Hull)
Intermeccanica – The Story of the Prancing Bull (McCredie & Reisner)
Italian Cafe Racers (Cloesen)
Italian Custom Motorcycles (Cloesen)
Jaguar E-type Racing Cars (Griffiths)
Jaguar, The Rise of (Price)
Jaguar XJ 220 – The Inside Story (Moreton)
Jaguar XJ-S, The Book of the (Long)
Japanese Custom Motorcycles – The Nippon Chop – Chopper, Cruiser, Bobber, Trikes and Quads (Cloesen)
Jeep CJ (Ackerson)
Jeep Wrangler (Ackerson)
The Jowett Jupiter – The car that leaped to fame (Nankivell)
Karmann-Ghia Coupé & Convertible (Bobbitt)
Kawasaki Triples Bible, The (Walker)
Kawasaki Z1 Story, The (Sheehan)
Kris Meeke – Intercontinental Rally Challenge Champion (McBride)
Lamborghini Miura Bible, The (Sackey)
Lamborghini Urraco, The Book of the (Landsem)
Lambretta Bible, The (Davies)
Lancia 037 (Collins)
Lancia Delta HF Integrale (Blaettel & Wagner)
Lancia Delta Integrale (Collins)
Land Rover Series III Reborn (Porter)
Land Rover, The Half-ton Military (Cook)
Laverda Twins & Triples Bible 1968-1986 (Falloon)
Lea-Francis Story, The (Price)
Le Mans Panoramic (Ireland)
Lexus Story, The (Long)
Little book of microcars, the (Quellin)
Little book of smart, the – New Edition (Jackson)
Little book of trikes, the (Quellin)
Lola – The Illustrated History (1957-1977) (Starkey)
Lola – All the Sports Racing & Single-seater Racing Cars 1978-1997 (Starkey)
Lola T70 – The Racing History & Individual Chassis Record – 4th Edition (Starkey)
Lotus 18 Colin Chapman's U-turn (Whitelock)
Lotus 49 (Oliver)
Marketingmobiles, The Wonderful Wacky World of (Hale)
Maserati 250F In Focus (Pritchard)
Mazda MX-5/Miata 1.6 Enthusiast's Workshop Manual (Grainger & Shoemark)
Mazda MX-5/Miata 1.8 Enthusiast's Workshop Manual (Grainger & Shoemark)
Mazda MX-5 Miata, The book of the – The 'Mk1' NA-series 1988 to 1997 (Long)
Mazda MX-5 Miata Roadster (Long)
Mazda Rotary-engined Cars (Cranswick)
Maximum Mini (Booij)
Meet the English (Bowie)
Mercedes-Benz SL – R230 series 2001 to 2011 (Long)
Mercedes-Benz SL – W113-series 1963-1971 (Long)
Mercedes-Benz SL & SLC – 107-series 1971-1989 (Long)
Mercedes-Benz SLK – R170 series 1996-2004 (Long)
Mercedes-Benz SLK – R171 series 2004-2011 (Long)
Mercedes-Benz W123-series – All models 1976 to 1986 (Long)
Mercedes G-Wagen (Long)
MGA (Price Williams)
MGB & MGB GT- Expert Guide (Auto-doc Series) (Williams)
MGB Electrical Systems Updated & Revised Edition (Astley)
Micro Caravans (Jenkinson)
Micro Trucks (Mort)
Microcars at Large! (Quellin)
Mini Cooper – The Real Thing! (Tipler)
Mini Minor to Asia Minor (West)
Mitsubishi Lancer Evo, The Road Car & WRC Story (Long)
Montlhéry, The Story of the Paris Autodrome (Boddy)
MOPAR Muscle - Barracuda, Dart & Valiant 1960-1980 (Cranswick)
Morgan Maverick (Lawrence)
Morgan 3 Wheeler – back to the future!, The (Dron)
Morris Minor, 60 Years on the Road (Newell)
Moto Guzzi Sport & Le Mans Bible, The (Falloon)
The Moto Guzzi Story - 3rd Edition (Falloon)
Motor Movies – The Posters! (Veysey)
Motor Racing – Reflections of a Lost Era (Carter)
Motor Racing – The Pursuit of Victory 1930-1962 (Carter)
Motor Racing – The Pursuit of Victory 1963-1972 (Wyatt/Sears)
Motor Racing Heroes – The Stories of 100 Greats (Newman)
Motorcycle Apprentice (Cakebread)
Motorcycle GP Racing in the 1960s (Pereira)
Motorcycle Road & Racing Chassis Designs (Noakes)
Motorcycling in the '50s (Clew)
Motorhomes, The Illustrated History (Jenkinson)
Motorsport In colour, 1950s (Wainwright)
MV Agusta Fours, The book of the classic (Falloon)
N.A.R.T. – A concise history of the North American Racing Team 1957 to 1983 (O'Neil)
Nissan 300ZX & 350Z – The Z-Car Story (Long)
Nissan GT-R Supercar: Born to race (Gorodji)
Northeast American Sports Car Races 1950-1959 (O'Neil)
Norton Commando Bible – All models 1968 to 1978 (Henshaw)
Nothing Runs – Misadventures in the Classic, Collectable & Exotic Car Biz (Slutsky)
Off-Road Giants! (Volume 1) – Heroes of 1960s Motorcycle Sport (Westlake)
Off-Road Giants! (Volume 2) – Heroes of 1960s Motorcycle Sport (Westlake)
Off-Road Giants! (Volume 3) – Heroes of 1960s Motorcycle Sport (Westlake)
Pass the Theory and Practical Driving Tests (Gibson & Hoole)
Peking to Paris 2007 (Young)
Pontiac Firebird – New 3rd Edition (Cranswick)
Porsche 356 (2nd Edition) (Long)
Porsche 908 (Födisch, Neßhöver, Roßbach, Schwarz & Roßbach)
Porsche 911 Carrera – The Last of the Evolution (Corlett)
Porsche 911R, RS & RSR, 4th Edition (Starkey)
Porsche 911, The Book of the (Long)
Porsche 911 – The Definitive History 2004-2012 (Long)
Porsche – The Racing 914s (Smith)
Porsche 911SC 'Super Carrera' – The Essential Companion (Streather)
Porsche 914 & 914-6: The Definitive History of the Road & Competition Cars (Long)
Porsche 924 (Long)
The Porsche 924 Carreras – evolution to excellence (Smith)
Porsche 928 (Long)
Porsche 944 (Long)
Porsche 964, 993 & 996 Data Plate Code Breaker (Streather)
Porsche 993 'King Of Porsche' – The Essential Companion (Streather)
Porsche 996 'Supreme Porsche' – The Essential Companion (Streather)
Porsche 997 2004-2012 – Porsche Excellence (Streather)
Porsche Boxster – The 986 series 1996-2004 (Long)
Porsche Boxster & Cayman - The 987 series (2004-2013) (Long)
Porsche Racing Cars – 1953 to 1975 (Long)
Porsche Racing Cars – 1976 to 2005 (Long)
Porsche – The Rally Story (Meredith)
Porsche: Three Generations of Genius (Meredith)
Powered by Porsche (Smith)
Preston Tucker & Others (Linde)
RAC Rally Action! (Gardiner)
Racing Colours – Motor Racing Compositions 1908-2009 (Newman)
Racing Line – British motorcycle racing in the golden age of the big single (Guntrip)
Rallye Sport Fords: The Inside Story (Moreton)
Renewable Energy Home Handbook, The (Porter)
Roads with a View - England's greatest views and how to find them by road (Corfield)
Rolls-Royce Silver Shadow/Bentley T Series Corniche & Camargue – Revised & Enlarged Edition (Bobbitt)
Rolls-Royce Silver Spirit, Silver Spur & Bentley Mulsanne 2nd Edition (Bobbitt)
Rootes Cars of the 50s, 60s & 70s – Hillman, Humber, Singer, Sunbeam & Talbot (Rowe)
Rover P4 (Bobbitt)
Runways & Racers (O'Neil)
Russian Motor Vehicles – Soviet Limousines 1930-2003 (Kelly)
Russian Motor Vehicles – The Czarist Period 1784 to 1917 (Kelly)
RX-7 – Mazda's Rotary Engine Sports car (Updated & Revised New Edition) (Long)
Scooters & Microcars, The A-Z of Popular (Dan)
Scooter Lifestyle (Grainger)
Scooter Mania! – Recollections of the Isle of Man International Scooter Rally (Jackson)
Singer Story: Cars, Commercial Vehicles, Bicycles & Motorcycle (Atkinson)
Sleeping Beauties USA – abandoned classic cars & trucks (Marek)
SM – Citroën's Maserati-engined Supercar (Long & Claverol)
Speedway – Auto racing's ghost tracks (Collins & Ireland)
Sprite Caravans, The Story of (Jenkinson)
Standard Motor Company, The Book of the (Robson)
Steve Hole's Kit Car Cornucopia – Cars, Companies, Stories, Facts & Figures: the UK's kit car scene since 1949 (Hole)
Subaru Impreza: The Road Car And WRC Story (Long)
Supercar, How to Build your own (Thompson)
Tales from the Toolbox (Oliver)
Tatra – The Legacy of Hans Ledwinka, Updated & Enlarged Collector's Edition of 1500 copies (Margolius & Henry)
Taxi! The Story of the 'London' Taxicab (Bobbitt)
This Day in Automotive History (Corey)
To Boldly Go – twenty six vehicle designs that dared to be different (Hull)
Toleman Story, The (Hilton)
Toyota Celica & Supra, The Book of Toyota's Sports Coupés (Long)
Toyota MR2 Coupés & Spyders (Long)
Triumph & Standard Cars 1945 to 1984 (Warrington)
Triumph Bonneville Bible (59-83) (Henshaw)
Triumph Bonneville!, Save the – The inside story of the Meriden Workers' Co-op (Rosamond)
Triumph Motorcycles & the Meriden Factory (Hancox)
Triumph Speed Twin & Thunderbird Bible (Woolridge)
Triumph Tiger Cub Bible (Estall)
Triumph Trophy Bible (Woolridge)
Triumph TR6 (Kimberley)
TT Talking – The TT's most exciting era – As seen by Manx Radio TT's lead commentator 2004-2012 (Lambert)
Two Summers – The Mercedes-Benz W196R Racing Car (Ackerson)
TWR Story, The – Group A (Hughes & Scott)
Unraced (Collins)
Velocette Motorcycles – MSS to Thruxton – New Third Edition (Burris)
Vespa - The Story of a Cult Classic in Pictures (Uhlig)
Vincent Motorcycles: The Untold Story since 1946 (Guyony & Parker)
Volkswagen Bus Book, The (Bobbitt)
Volkswagen Bus or Van to Camper, How to Convert (Porter)
Volkswagens of the World (Glen)
VW Beetle Cabriolet – The full story of the convertible Beetle (Bobbitt)
VW Beetle – The Car of the 20th Century (Copping)
VW Bus – 40 Years of Splitties, Bays & Wedges (Copping)
VW Bus Book, The (Bobbitt)
VW Golf: Five Generations of Fun (Copping & Cservenka)
VW – The Air-cooled Era (Copping)
VW T5 Camper Conversion Manual (Porter)
VW Campers (Copping)
Volkswagen Type 3, The book of the - Concept, Design, International Production Models & Development (Glen)
Volvo Estate, The (Hollebone)
You & Your Jaguar XK8/XKR – Buying, Enjoying, Maintaining, Modifying – New Edition (Thorley)
Which Oil? – Choosing the right oils & greases for your antique, vintage, veteran, classic or collector car (Michell)
Wolseley Cars 1948 to 1975 (Rowe)
Works Minis, The Last (Purves & Brenchley)
Works Rally Mechanic (Moylan)

WWW.VELOCE.CO.UK

First published in 2001 by Veloce Publishing Limited, Veloce House, Parkway Farm Business Park, Middle Farm Way, Poundbury, Dorchester DT1 3AR, England. Fax 01305 268864 / e-mail info@veloce.co.uk / web www.veloce.co.uk or www.velocebooks.com.
Reprinted 2004, 2007, September 2015 & March 2018.
ISBN: 978-1-845848-70-5/UPC: 6-36847-04870-9
© 2001, 2004, 2007, 2015 and 2018 Brian Moylan and Veloce Publishing Ltd.

All rights reserved. With the exception of quoting brief passages for the purpose of review, no part of this publication may be recorded, reproduced or transmitted by any means, including photocopying, without the written permission of Veloce Publishing. Throughout this book logos, model names and designations, etc., may have been used for the purposes of identification, illustration and decoration. Such names are the property of the trademark holder as this is not an official publication. Readers with ideas for automotive books, or books on other transport or related hobby subjects, are invited to write to Veloce Publishing at the above address.
British Library Cataloguing in Publication Data -
A catalogue record for this book is available from the British Library.
Typesetting, design and page make-up all by Veloce on AppleMac. Printed and bound by CPI Group (UK) Ltd, Croydon, CR0 4YY.

ANATOMY OF THE
WORKS MINIS

BRIAN MOYLAN

VELOCE PUBLISHING
THE PUBLISHER OF FINE AUTOMOTIVE BOOKS

Contents

Chapter 1. In the Beginning . 7

Chapter 2. Bodyshell and Instruments 17

Chapter 3. Subframes and Suspension 30

Chapter 4. Footbrakes 33

Chapter 5. 'Fly-off' Handbrake 34

Chapter 6. Steering 37

Chapter 7. Wheels 39

Chapter 8. Engine 43

Chapter 9. Gearbox 49

Chapter 10. Electrics 51

Chapter 11. Fuel System 56

Chapter 12. Miscellaneous .. 59

Chapter 13. The Moment of Truth 63

Appendix A. The Racing Mini 67
   Suspension modifications on a Mini racer 67
   The Mini racing engine ... 69
   Fuel injection 72
   The dry sump 73
   The limited-slip differential 74
   Tyres 74
   Accessory modifications . 75
   Racing successes 76
   The Works racers 78

Appendix B. The Rallycross Mini 80
   Joining the works team .. 80
   Life after Comps closed ... 84
   The quest for more power 85
   Suspension mods 86
   Four-wheel drive 87

Index 94

Introduction

When I first saw the Job Sheet that is the basis for this book, I had the idea that it would make an interesting magazine article. My approach to one of the Mini magazines brought the reply that there was probably enough material to fill a book, which they encouraged me to write. So here it is.

As I began to prepare the book I realised that no description of a particular Mini could adequately represent the many and divers developments that contributed to the make-up of the Mini's anatomy. It is this fact that caused me to go beyond the confines of the Job Sheet to describe work carried out when a Mini would be entered into a rally in a different category, or a special event like a marathon, a race or a rallycross. Each would bring its own special problems, most of which would be sorted out by the factory's design office. Many details, however, were up to the individual mechanic who drew his ideas on the back of the proverbial fag packet.

This book is not meant as a Workshop Manual, but as an explanation of why and how individual jobs were carried out. It may come as a surprise to some that arguably the most successful rally car of all time came about with the aid of a 'knife and fork' rather than a computer; with the occasional use of a spoon to stir things up a bit.

Job satisfaction was not a phrase that was used in the sixties, certainly not in a car factory where the majority of employees were completing the same ten minute task over and over again. Going to work, for many, was just to earn a living. However, to be given a car to strip out, rebuild, test, and follow no matter where in the world it would be sent, to take part in one of the most exciting sports in the world was job satisfaction indeed.

Brian Moylan, Abingdon

Acknowledgements

The memories, ideas and thoughts of many people have gone into the writing of this book. First there was Bill Price, who started it by giving me the Job Sheet from which I had worked to build the Mini Cooper S for Tony Fall and Henry Lidden to drive on the 1966 German Rally. His advice and guidance has been of great help.

I have also been fortunate to have fellow mechanics Den Green, Tommy Wellman and Cliff Humphreys, designer Terry Mitchell, Basil Wales (ex-BMC/BL Special Tuning Manager, 1965-74), and Peter Browning, the Competitions Manager, all delving into their memories of long gone days.

From beyond the factory gates has come support from the late John Cooper, Ginger Devlin, Jeff Williamson and Tom Seal.

Photographs from all of these sources have been invaluable, as has the Photographic Archive of the BMIHT at Gaydon.

Drawings were made by ex-MG apprentice and Son-in-Law Michael Sibbald.

Half forgotten memories have been brought to the surface by reading the books of Marcus Chambers, Stuart Turner, Bill Price and Peter Browning.

My thanks to all of these and to Rod Grainger of Veloce Publishing for having the faith to put my words into print.

Chapter 1
In the Beginning

The rally winning Mini Cooper 'S' didn't just come into being overnight. It evolved over a period of ten years, beginning with the 850cc shopping car of 1959. Incidentally, 1959 was the year that the car made its competition debut when three cars were entered in the RAC Rally. All three, however, retired with slipping clutches. Through trial and error under rally conditions, and through rigorous testing by the mechanics in the BMC Competitions Department, the car developed into the 1275 racer of 1969.

The cars that came off the production line in Longbridge underwent a very radical metamorphosis when taken to Abingdon for rally preparation. The department that wrought this transformation had been brought into being in 1955 by John Thornley, the Managing Director of the MG Car Company.

The man in charge in those early days, however, was Marcus Chambers. Under his management the Competition Department split from the MG Development and Experimental Department, within which the former had come into being, and was moulded into an efficient and independent unit.

Much of Marcus' success was due to the Austin-Healey that his department brought to international rally winning standard on some of the most gruelling events in the calendar. Little was it realised that the mantle carried by this 3000cc six cylinder monster, with its three twin-choke Weber carburettors, would soon be taken over by a tiny tin box with a Morris Minor engine, fitted in sideways, driving the front wheels.

When the cars were unloaded from the transporter that brought them to Abingdon from the Austin factory in Longbridge, Birmingham, they were taken into the workshop in 'B' Block, separated from the main factory ('A' Block with its MG production lines) by a wide tarmac 'yard.'

Anatomy of the Works Minis

In the Beginning

Timo Makinen's 1965 Monte winner. Or is it?

The workshop was one of the buildings erected during the 1939-45 war to produce tanks and aircraft parts. This workshop was the first in a block of similar buildings and was identified by the number 'B1.' Crusader tanks had been built here during the war

Opposite top: The building that housed the Competition Department was across the 'yard', remote from the main factory.

Opposite bottom: The overhead crane installed for wartime tank production could easily cope with a Mini.

and a 20 ton overhead travelling crane was a legacy of those days. Some of the staff were instructed in the art of driving this monster. Tony Bramley, for example, one of Neville Challis' storemen, became quite skilled in manipulating it and, from the cabin high in the workshop roof, he could install the tiny Mini engine to within an inch of its resting place with the aid of hand signals from the mechanic.

It was customary for new cars to be delivered for use on the

Monte Carlo Rally, this being the first event of the year. Although often completely overhauled, re-engined, and sometimes rebodied, the car would then be used on events throughout the coming year. If a car won the 'Monte', however, it became a showpiece car, clones of which would then appear as the Monte Carlo Rally winning Mini in BMC showrooms throughout the UK.

A 'build sheet' had been devised, covering ten foolscap pages, with headings that dealt

Anatomy of the Works Minis

with every aspect of the car's preparation. Doug Watts, the Department Supervisor, and his two foremen, Tommy Wellman and Den Green, would fill in the details appropriate to the event and category for which the car was being prepared. Tom or Den would then come into the workshop and hand this build sheet to the mechanic who was going to be responsible for carrying out the job.

The new car, so recently assembled on the Longbridge production lines, underwent immediate disassembly (including removal of the engine, subframes, doors and bootlid).

Disassembling a standard car and starting from scratch was preferable to trying to order a complete car, with its dozens of brackets, screws, bolts, and other items, piecemeal. Stripping it of the major components only took a day to complete and the conversion to a rally car could begin.

Date	July 66	Event	German Rally	Cat. & Group	II
Car Type	Engine No.		Chassis No.	Comp. No.	Mechanic
	9F-SA-Y K0617		GA2S7 821287		B. MOYLAN
JBL 172D	Austin Cooper 'S'				T. FALL / H. LIDDON

Cylinder Block		
Bore size	✓	+ .020"
Modified	✓	MACHINE FACE TO .010" OFF PISTON CROWN
Fume pipes	✓	STD BLANK OFF CLACK VALVE CUT HOLES IN NOSE
Camshaft	✓	AEA 648 ?
Crankshaft	✓	Balanced double drilled & blanked off as drawing 707/823 STD
Flywheel	✓	SPL LIGHTENED & BALANCED USE SPECIAL LINING TOOL
Clutch	✓	REINFORCED Diaphragm (orange) balanced WITH SPL. THRUST PAD
Release bearing	✓	STD repack with HMP grease
Bearings cam	✓	STD
Bearings crank		SPL Vandervell
Con rods	✓	STD line up and balance MACHINE GROOVE IN RODS BOLTS .003 STRETCH
Pistons		+.020" SPL PISTONS MACHINE EXTRA OIL HOLE IN BOSS
Oil pump	✓	STD CONCENTRIC
Oil pump drive	✓	STD
Camshaft gear		MACHINE TO LINE UP & LIGHTEN
Crankshaft gear		STD " " " " & "
Timing chain		STD RENEW
Core plugs	✓	Isopan around edges of core plugs
Dip stick & washer		Blue dipstick and check length
Oil filter element		Re-new
Distributor		40979B & latest condensor & rotor arm grease point pivot
Ignition setting		Test on rolling road and report
Engine rubbers		LATEST STD TYPE 2 REAR TYPE
Check engine No. Plate		Yes
Idler gear	✓	STD
Primary gear		SPL Vandervell steel back bush STD
Oil pressure		Check and report
Sump & protection		MAX FULL PROTECTION. PLUS MINI MOKE SHEILD. FIT PROTECTION BRACKETS TO TIE ROD EYES
Oil cooler		ARO.9809 with SPL flex pipes, check for fouling
		Modify engine steady bracket bush at bulkhead end
		Fit spacer and bolt for ease of removal

MODIFY OIL COOLER MOUNTING & FRONT STEADY BRACKET TO CLEAR ALTERNATOR
FIT LIGHTENED BASE TAPPETS

The illustrations on the following pages are reproduced from a ten-page rally car build sheet.

In the Beginning

- 2 -

Cylinder Head		LOCKTIGHT Centre pop, 3 blanks in centre of cyl. head
Type		DOWNTON
Modified	✓	CHECK FOR 6 BRASS PLUGS DE-SAND WATER WAYS.
Compression ratio	✓	12.6-1
Amount removed		BY DOWNTON.
Combustion space	✓	16.4 cc
Exhaust valves	✓	STD
Inlet valves	✓	STD, Mod. DOWNTON.
Top caps		Marked W
Bottom caps		AEA 654
Valve spring inner	✓	AEA.652 CHECK PRESSURES.
Valve spring outer	✓	AEA.524
Thermostat	✓	BLANK BY-PASS USE THERMOSTAT TOP PLATE ONLY
~~Sealing points~~		Nil
Exhaust manifold		DOWNTON.
Inlet manifold		DOWNTON
Plugs		N60Y
Rocker assembly		FIT LATEST TYPE REMOVE .055" FROM PILLARS FIT MODIFIED SHAFT DRILL & COUNTERSINK PLAIN PILLAR FOR OILWAY LINE UP ROCKER ARM WITH VALVE STEM

- 3 -

Transmission

Gear ratios	✓	C/R
Gear material	✓	SPL crack tested
Type of transmission	✓	Spur cut gears
Sump plug	✓	STD
Selector bars & forks	✓	Check and tighten
Dip stick		Nil BLUE END CHECK FOR LENGTH
Filler cap mods.	✓	Check DRILL HOLES IN SLOT OF FILLER CAP.
Check oil leaks		CHECK.
Gear lever	STD	~~Old type fit new for antirattle~~ (check ease of change)
Drive shafts	✓	SPL latest modified type from Hardy Spicer
Propshafts		Latest type Hardy Spicer needle roller
Diff. ratio	✓	4.26-1 SPL CHECKED.
Clutch adjustment	✓	STD.
Sump protection		Full protection + MINI MOKE
~~Rear axle casing~~	✗	Nil
Half shafts		Fit enlarged diam. shafts FLANGE BOLT 50 LBS FT.
Overdrive		NIL.
REMOTE CONTROL MOUNTING		FIT MITCHELL RUBBER. STRENGTHEN MOUNTING. REMOVE PLATE FROM BODY TO USE FOR STRENGTHENING

Carburettors

Type of carburettors	✓	Twin 1¼
Modified	✓	FLOAT CHAMBER EXT.
Needles		BG
Dash pot springs		BLUE
Dampers	✓	AUC 8103.
Air cleaners	✓	FIT STUB PIPES LESS BREATHER
Choke cables	✓	STD
Heat shields		Fit asbestos to bulkhead under bonnet
Heat collecting box		Yes make and fit
~~Thermo heating~~		Nil
Induction	✓	DOWNTON.
Linkage	✓	Fork and peg LINE UP.
Cable accel.		SPL nylon insert Smiths check aligment
Float level		Check with ext.
Vibration		Check
		Wire lock banjo bolts to float chamber bolts

Anatomy of the Works Minis

Chassis		
Front ~~springs~~ PISTON ✓		FIT LONGER OLD TYPE. CARE ON FITTING
Rear ~~springs~~ PISTON ✓		STD SHORT TYPE. " " "
~~Packing rings~~	×	NIL.
Displacer units	✓	Double ~~Blue~~ rear, single ~~Blue~~ front
~~Struts front~~	✓	Nil
Struts rear	✓	STD ORANGE WITH 30LB HELPER SPRINGS.
~~Anti roll bars~~		Nil
~~Anti roll bar links~~		Nil
~~Rear shackles~~		Nil
Wishbones	✓	STD ~~mod~~ LATEST TYPE RUBBERS
Bump rubbers	✓	SPL AEON RUBBERS AS MGB.
U bolts		SPL
~~Front shockers~~		Nil
~~Rear shockers~~		Nil
~~Torsion bars~~		Nil
Chassis strengthening	✓	STRENGTHEN REAR SWING ARM BRACKETS.
Chassis mods	✓	DOUBLE SKIN TOP OF REAR SUB FRAME.
Engine mounting brkts		STD.
~~Shocker mounting brkts~~		Nil
Bumpers	✓	STD
Jacking points	✓	Quick lift. Brackets front and rear
Height of car		STD APPROX 13" WHEEL CENTRE TO WHEEL ARCH
Front hubs		STD checked and packed with H207/62 grease
Rear hubs	✓	SPL Timken from T. & T. with H207/62 grease THESE ARE NOW STD STRIP & REPACK.
Stub axles	✓	STD
Towing eyes	✓	TWO Front
~~Overriders~~	✓	Nil REMOVE
Radius arms	✓	STD
Tie rods	✓	Split pin nuts FIT NEW RUBBERS.
Lubricate		Well
Fog lamp brkts		Fit quick release type HEAVIER BRKT. AT CENTRE.

- 5 -

Cooling System	✓	Fit radiator DEV 3023 BOLT SOLID AT BOTTOM END
Type of fan	✓	Fit 4 bladed WITH MACHINED ENDS.
Type of radiator	✓	16 gills per inch with ¼" AF fixing screws MOD COWLING
Water pump	✓	SMALL STD pulley
Hoses	✓	STD
Fan belt	✓	MINTEX
~~Radiator blind~~		Nil
Blanking	✓	BY PASS IN WATER PUMP.
~~Anti freeze~~		NIL.
Rad cap	✓	13 lbs. WIRED ON.
Header tank	✓	STD
Temp. gauge		SPL Smiths CAPILARY TUBE ARMOURED.
Rad. drain plug		Wire lock
Rad. drain tap		Wire lock
Flush system		Yes

MAX CLEARENCE RAD TO BODY COWL.

In the Beginning

- 6 -

Electrics	
Alternator	Fit & MODIFY EARTH WIRE
Starter ✓	STD RT 25110
Coil	HA 12 AND WATER PROOF
Reg. box	For alternator 4 TR 37423 A
Battery & fixing	MONTY type fitted with terminals away from petrol tank
Alternator pulley	AEA.535
Water proofing	Silicone grease, rubber covers on coil & distributor & alloy plate in front
~~AUXILIARY LAMPS FRONT~~	FIT SNAP CONNECTORS FOR QUICK REMOVAL
~~Overdrive switch~~	Nil
Wiper motor	TWO SPEED.
Wiper motor switch	TWO SPEED FITTED DRIVERS PANEL.
Wiper blades & arms	STD fit deep throated wheel boxes
Headlamps	EUROPEAN E4 (WHITE)
Headlamp bulbs	VERTICAL DIP 60/40
Fog lamps	Two 700 latest type fitted with iodine bulbs TWO WITH H/L UNIT
Fog lamp switch	One for each light
Fog lamp bulbs	Iodine
Long range lamps	TWO FITTED WITH H/L UNITS.
Long range switch	TWO CENTRE WITH H/L UNITS INCORPERATED WITH MAIN BEAM
Long range bulb	IODINE.
Reverse lamp	STD A/H SIDE LAMP. LOW DOWN.
Reverse lamp switch	FITTED TO GEARBOX
Reverse lamp bulb	12v 21w
Tail lamps ✓	STD
Stop lamps ✓	STD
Flasher lamps ✓	STD
Flasher switch ✓	STD POSITION. INCORPERATED WITH SIDE LIGHTS
2 pin plugs ✓	One in glove pocket 2nd compartment back from front
Navigators lamps ✓	Butlers flex type in glove pocket FACING REAR
~~Demister bars~~	Nil
Lamp covers	All front lamps
Horns	Maserati
Horn buttons ✓	STD for driver foot operated for passenger
Panel lights ✓	STD
Panel light rev. counter	STD
Panel light speedo	STD
Panel light odometer	STD
Panel light clocks	External 4 LIGHTS. WITH EXT
Focus lamps	Yes
~~Ammeter~~	Nil
H/lamp flick switch ✓	Fit
Battery	Make up and fit cover
Battery cable	Fit large type terminal covers to insulate and run inside car
Screen washer elec.	Lucas electric. Fit switch to drivers panel

FIT NON RETURN VALVE INSIDE BOTTLE
TO KEEP VERTICAL
FIT CHROME JETS

Anatomy of the Works Minis

- 7 -

6. contd.

~~Headlamp washers~~		Nil
	✓	Fit 2 cigar lighters on drivers and navigators side
Steering	✓	Fit modified U bolt to location side of rack
Type of column		STD check bottom clamp bolt & LINE UP
Type of steering wheel	✓	Leather covered LATEST TYPE. WITH THUMB PADS.
Steering wheel nut		Tighten MATT BLACK SPOKES
Rack & pinion	✓	STD fit vulcolen bush and shim to .003
Steering arms		STD latest type STRIP CLEAN & LAP FACES
~~Steering idler~~		Nil
Track arms		STD split pin nuts CHECK FIT OF TAPER
Camber & caster		Check
Lubricate		Well
Lock nuts		Fit castellated nuts & split pin both ends of the rods
Steering ratio	✓	STD
Adjustment		Check
Line up steering wheel		Yes
Track wheels		1/8" toe out
		Fit SPL ball pins SK 21556
Exhaust		FIT SKID UNDER SILENCER & TURN UP TAIL PIPE
Type of system		COMPETITION. TYPE.
Type of silencer		" "
Hanging brkts		SPL DRILL RUBBER FIT BOLTS. (DO NOT
Support brkt. front		SPL
Fit steel exh. clips in place of Jubilee clips and weld on		FIT LOCKING BAR TO EACH JOIN
Petrol System		
Tank		FIT 2.
Tank fixing		STD. ~~Fit strap to outside of tank~~
Fuel gauge		STD with Bi-metal strip
Pumps	✓	TWIN PUMP UNDER REAR SEAT (WIRE ONE ONLY)
Pipes	✓	RUN INSIDE CAR.
Tank fillers		STD WIRE OUTSIDE.
Tank protection		ASBESTOS shield
Pipe protection	✓	INSIDE CAR.
Heat protection		N/A
Leaks		Check
Petrol filters		Clean
Tank breather		STD. CHECK FOR CLEARANCE. CHECK OUTLETS ARE CLEAR.

TANK PIPES ✓ — MODIFY THREE WAY CONNECTOR BETWEEN.
TANKS AS STD ONE NOT GOOD ENOUGH.

In the Beginning

- 8 -

FIT MODIFIED SEAT BRACKETS.

Body NAVIGATORS SEAT.	SPL LET DOWN, FIT STRAPS TO LOCATE HARNESS
Drivers seat SPECIAL PADDING	FIBRE GLASS. SPREAD WITH PORTA POWER.
Drivers harness	SPL Irvin lamp and diagonal
Passengers harness	SPL Irvin full harness
W/screen ✓	Laminated
W/screen washers ✓	Lucas electric FIT NON RETURN VALVE IN BOTTLE.
Sun visors	STD latest type
Perspex windows	Nil
Snow deflector	Nil
Perspex heat shield	Nil
Rear window wiper	Nil
Demist	Fit clear view HIGH AS POSSIBLE
Cold air system	Nil
Heater FIT MOUNTING BRKT WITH SPACER	Yes STD fit larger diam. demister pipes WITH FUNNEL
Vents in wings	Nil
Vents in roof	Nil
Front wings ✓	STD FIT FIBRE GLASS SPATS & POP RIVET FINISHER
Rear wings ✓	STD " " " " "
Doors ✓	STD POP RIVET PLASTIC FINISHER ON INSIDE OF DOORS
Panels	STD
Fairings ✓	STD remove over-riders
Bonnet ✓	STD
Bonnet fixings ✓	STD fix straps
Doors for shut	Check
Safety catches	Check
Hard top	N/A
Hard top fixings	N/A
Crash bars	N/A
Window fixings ✓	STD check
Carpets	STD insulate with asbestos blanket underneath front
Trim	STD
Map stowage ✓	Divide N/S door pocket
Parcel shelf	Nil
Door draughts	Check and rectify
Water test	Check and rectify
Paddings	Fit to door pocket locks and pillars & rear of N/S door pocket
Facia	SPL made in Comps. MATT BLACK ALL CHROME
Switch position	Arrange as instructed. Fitted to drivers panel W/washer
Thermos	Nil & W/wiper
Body	STICK up bung holes in floor & SEAL.
	Cut holes in rear panel for removing spring as for S/S
	Modify boot lid catch

FIT RUBBER STRAP TO BOOTLID.
FIT INTER COM BOX &
MAKE UP & FIT EMERGENCY STRAP FOR REMOTE CONTROL.

Anatomy of the Works Minis

```
- 9 -
```

Body - contd.

Registratio Nos.	FRONT Stick on fablon	FIAT MADE UP Nº PLATE AT REAR
G.B.	Yes	
Comp. Nos.	Painted matt. black	
Eolopress ✓	Yes fit	
Fire extinguisher ✓	Yes fit	
Driving mirror ✓	STD LATEST MINI ARM (WITH LARGE SUCKER) MGB GT. MIRROR.	
Passengers mirror	Barnacle	
Petrol can stowage	Nil	
Kit stowage	Yes as much as possible	
Scotchlite tape	Rear bumpers and door shuts	
Grab handles	Fit one above passengers door	
Safety fast	Yes	
Union jacks	Yes	
Rally plates	Yes	
NAME PLATES.	LATEST STICK ON TYPE	

```
- 10 -
```

Controls

Accel. pedal ✓		Modify for toe and heel
Accel. pedal brkts. ✓	STD.	Modify for toe and heel
Accel. cable ✓		Nylon insert Smiths line up for ease
Accel. linkage ✓		Fork and peg
Brake pedal ✓		STD
Pedal box ✓		STD
Clutch pedal ✓		STD
H/brake lever ✓		Modify for fly off
H/brake cables		Grease well USE P.B.C. ON PIVOT POINTS.

Instruments

Speedo	KPH with trip
Trip instrument	Halda twinmeter
Cables	Halda SPL bar
Halda	As above
Clocks	2 off Heuer
R/counters	Smiths electric
R/counter cables	Nil
Safety gauge	Yes
Ignition key	Yes and spares
Boot key	Yes and spares
Ice thermometer	No

Tyres & Wheels

Type of tyre	R 7 ?
Tubes	Yes
Spare wheels	Four ?
Valve caps	Yes
Balance	Yes
Wheel	Wide rims

Chapter 2
Bodyshell and Instruments

The shell became the first focus of attention. Stripped of its windscreen and rear window, instruments, wiring loom, seats, headlining and other trim, the tiresome job of removing the weighty sound deadening felt from inside the roof could begin.

This was carried out by pulling off as much as would easily come away and applying solvent to melt the adhesive holding the rest, then scraping and mopping to remove all traces. This solvent was quite toxic and using it in the confined space soon started

Extended and strengthened seat brackets.

Anatomy of the Works Minis

Two inch lightening holes cut in the rear bulkhead.

Bodyshell and Instruments

The windscreen washer bottle was brought inside the car.

the senses reeling, whereupon it was a case of staggering to the workshop door for a few lungfuls of fresh air. More weight-saving exercises were carried out when the car was running in a category that permitted them. On the 1965 Monte Mini, for instance, the rear bulkhead had a series of 2 inch holes cut in it. Later regulations, which required the boot containing the petrol tanks to be sealed

The Mini in its BMC livery of red and white nears completion.

from the cockpit, would have forbidden this method.

The major body strength-ening was the addition of a specially pressed crossmember that carried the front seat mountings. The Mini body had shown signs of starting to fold in half, with a crease appearing where the crossmember went over the tunnel. This additional item was a replica of the original but just sufficiently larger for it to be fitted over the original and welded in place, thus rendering it safe from detection were some pedantic

scrutineer to consider such an addition to be inadmissible. Before proceeding further the bare body was taken to the paint shop to be painted in the team colour, red with the white roof and white patches on the doors where the vinyl rally number would later be stuck on.

The seat mounting brackets were modified, by extending them backwards, to provide more adjustment. The seats them-selves were to be replaced; the driver's by a fibreglass seat

Anatomy of the Works Minis

Electric defrosters on the 1963 Monte Carlo rally car, crewed by Paddy Hopkirk and Jack Scott.

that was padded to the driver's requirements (with the extra padding it was necessary to spread the seat with a body jack). The navigator had a special reclining seat – a vast im-provement over the Heath Robinson contraptions that we made in the workshop before proper ones were available. Straps fitted to the sides of the navigator's seat held the safety harness in place so that if the navigator had to jump out to use a time clock at a control there was no fumbling for the belt when he, or she, leapt back in. The safety harness itself had to be fitted (they were not legally required before 1967, so mounting points were not in the car as standard).

The old squirter windscreen washer was discarded in favour of a Lucas electrical model, which, according to the build sheet, did not have a non-return valve so there would be an aggravating delay between pushing the button and solvent squirting on the screen. The instruction was to fit a valve on the end of the tube in the bottle

Bodyshell and Instruments

Timo Makinen looking pleased with the padding covering the door lock and sharp edges on the door.

to overcome this. The bottle was considerably larger than the standard one and there was no room for it under the bonnet, so it was brought inside and fixed to the inner wing beside the navigator's left foot.

With regard to sunvisors, the build sheet says: "standard latest type." What it doesn't say is that the production method of fixing the visor was with a self tapping screw. This screw would come loose and had been known to fall out. It is not possible to get behind the panel to use a nut and bolt so we used what we called 'Aero' type nuts. These were 10UNF nuts with wings for fixing into position. So, a hole was drilled in place of the self-tapper hole, of a size to allow the nut to be pushed in leaving the wings on the outside of the panel to be held in place by pop rivets.

The demister ducts on the heater were modified with larger diameter pipes and 'funnels' to spread the air on to the screen for more efficient demisting. In the early days a Monte Carlo rally car would have a four inch wide strip of perspex fitted across the top of the dashboard in an effort to hold the hot air against the screen and improve demisting, with an additional Lucas electric defroster bar fixed to the screen by suckers. Electrically heated windscreens were introduced much later.

Anatomy of the Works Minis

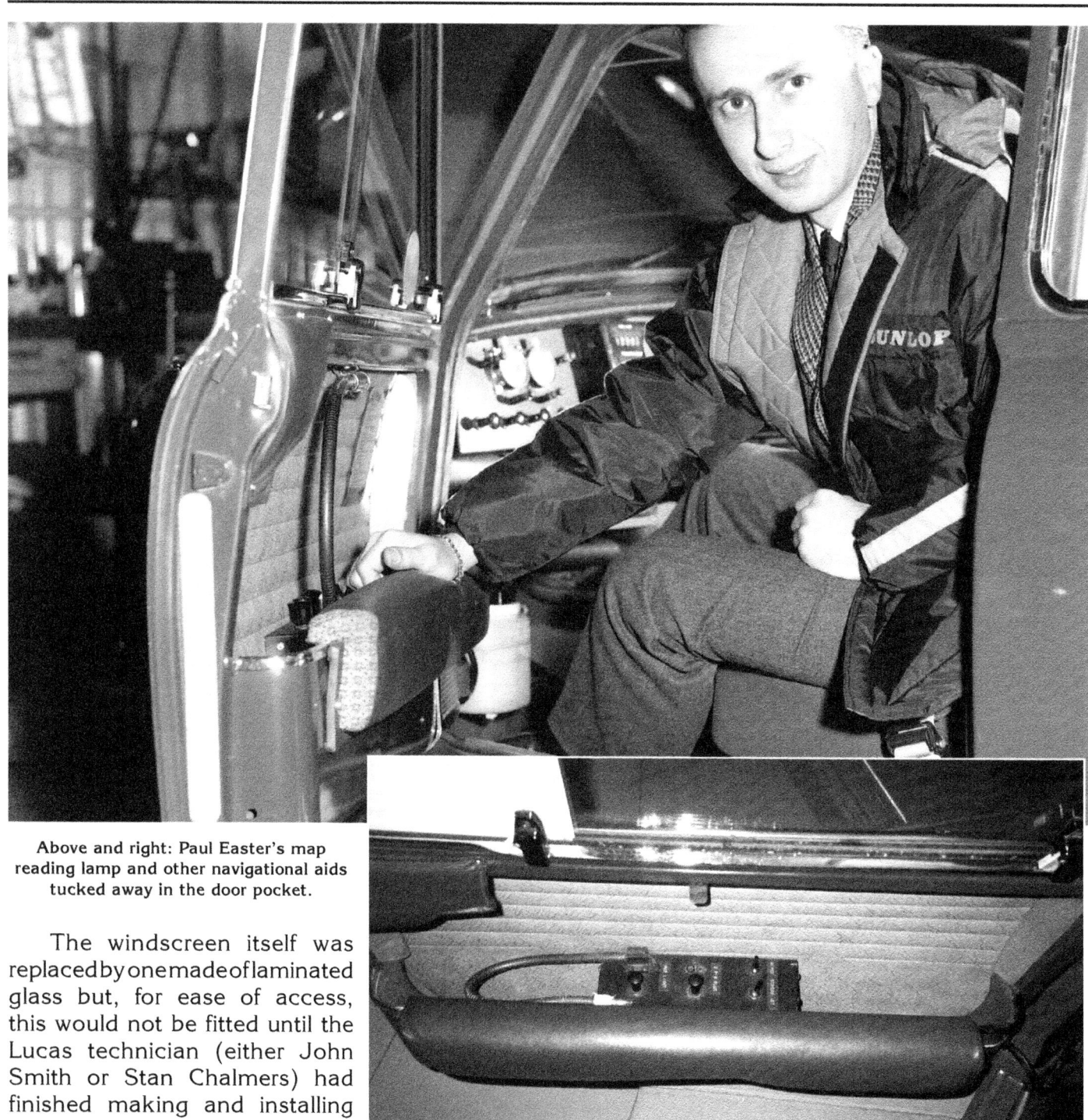

Above and right: Paul Easter's map reading lamp and other navigational aids tucked away in the door pocket.

The windscreen itself was replaced by one made of laminated glass but, for ease of access, this would not be fitted until the Lucas technician (either John Smith or Stan Chalmers) had finished making and installing the wiring harness. The rear window demisting was taken care of by a 'Clearview' panel. This was a panel of transparent

Bodyshell and Instruments

Everything shiny, including the roof lining, was covered with matt black paint.

material approximately 12ins by 24ins on a quarter inch thick rubber frame that adhered to the window making what amounted to a double-glazed space which always stayed clear.

Where the regulations allowed, the windows were replaced by perspex ones and the opening rear side windows were discarded in favour of perspex held in by rubber seals. Otherwise, all that could be done to the windows was to make sure that the catches on the front door windows operated efficiently.

The sound deadening under the door trim was removed. The plastic finisher on the door pocket had to be pop riveted more securely and the pocket was padded to soften possible contact with the crews' elbows. More padding was applied to the door locks and the door shut pillar. Individual drivers, of course, often had their own requests for padding. The outside of a long legged driver's right knee could get chaffed if he was in the habit of bracing his leg against the bodywork, so placing a pad here was another instance of the car being 'made to measure'. The door pocket on the navigator's side was partitioned to provide

23

Anatomy of the Works Minis

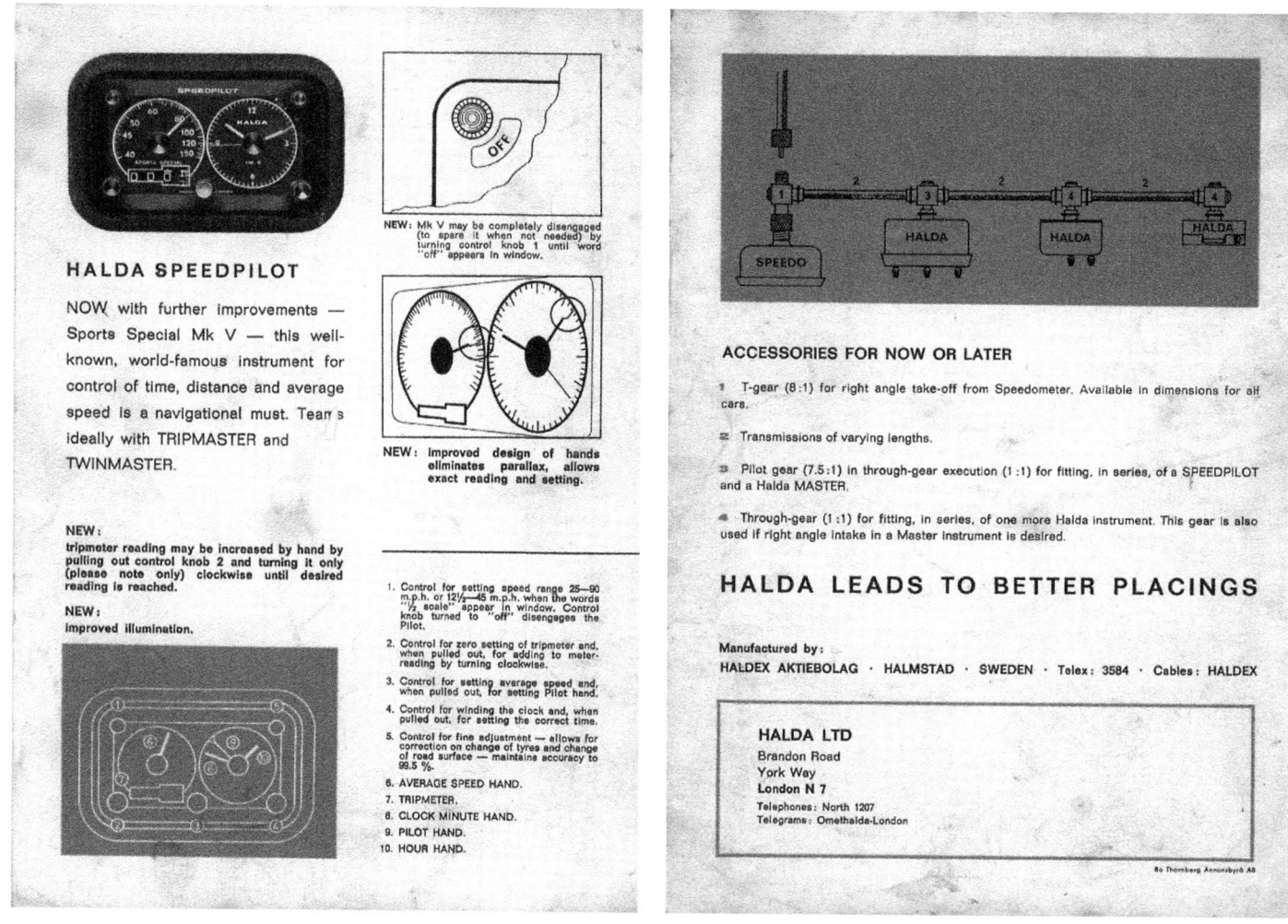

The Halda Speedpilot average speed indicator (left), and the Halda drive off the speedo cable.

storage for the maps. A 'Butler' long flexible map reading light was attached to the door and a two-pin plug was wired in for the navigator to plug in his own magnifier map light.

The headlining was painted matt black before being refitted. The same treatment was given to all of the chrome bezels of the instruments, which were mounted in the special instrument panels made by Stan Bradford, the shop panel-beater, and painted crackle black in the factory paint shop. The illumination lights in the instruments were controlled by a dimmer switch.

A pair of Heuer clocks were mounted on the navigator's instrument panel. These were illuminated by small pedestal lights which emitted a red glow and were of a type used to illuminate aircraft instruments. All of these measures were, of course, designed to aid the driver's night vision.

The early navigation aid was the Halda average speed indicator, called the 'Speedpilot,' which had to be adjusted to give an accurate reading over a known distance. A circuit round the Frilford Golf Course, starting and finishing at the 'Dog House' pub, was exactly 9.6 kilometres (6 miles). This was the reading that the odometer on the Speedpilot had to show – any more and the adjusting screw had to be turned back,

Bodyshell and Instruments

HALDA TRIPMASTER

Small in size, great in accuracy and performance, the specification details all the exciting features of the HALDAS. The great combination for distance and average speed: TRIPMASTER + SPEEDPILOT.

HALDA ARE PROUD TO MANUFACTURE FINE RALLY INSTRUMENTS. THEY HAVE BEEN CREATED, TESTED AND REFINED IN CLOSE COOPERATION BETWEEN TOP TEAMS AND HALDA, ENTITLING US TO REGARD THEM AS THE IDEAL INSTRUMENTS, MADE TO YOUR REQUIREMENTS FOR BETTER RESULTS AND YOUR GREATER SATISFACTION.

ADDITIONAL SPECIFICATION FOR TWINMASTER ONLY

COUNTERS
Twin-counters, each with the same specification as above.

INSTANT 0-SETTING
Separate for each counter.

COUNTER GEAR-SHIFT
This can be set in one of three positions:
a. so that both counters work **simultaneously**: one for total distance, one for specials
b. so that counters work **one at a time** with quick-switch between them. The figure for a leg just completed, may consequently be retained whilst the other counter registers the new leg.

FOR CHECKING OF OTHER INSTRUMENTS
Due to their great accuracy (achieved through the trimming gear + the 1/100 mile-wheel) HALDA's two Master Instruments are suitable for precision checking of for instance Speedpilots, Taximeters and the standard car odometers. The precision of the Master Instruments themselves may be checked over a short (1/10—2/10 of a mile is enough), accurately measured distance.

EXTRA ACCESSORIES
1. Complete gear for quick-change (pre-adapted to deal for instance with change of tyres).
2. Gear wheels, with teeth well protected by roller. The centre tube is cut according to the number of wheels, which are to be kept on the roller.

HALDA TWINMASTER

This instrument is designed to give all the answers on accurate distance measuring. All mechanical, silent precision instrument. Unique + 0 — gear permits correct distance reading on return to point of error after erroneous detour. Unique twin counters with gearshift giving the invaluable facility of simultaneous or alternate work as required.
From the specification it will be realised that the HALDA TWINMASTER is the most resourceful and the most all round competition instrument now available.
The perfect team for distance and average speed: TWINMASTER + SPEEDPILOT.

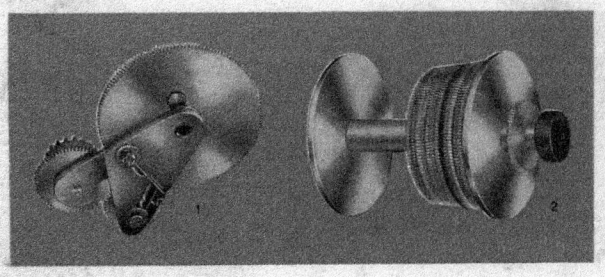

Left: Halda Twinmaster for accurate distance measurement. Right: Two hundred and ninety eight combinations of gear wheels ensure accurate calibration of the Speedpilot.

any less and the screw had to be turned forward. It could take quite a few trips round the circuit to get it just right. In use the Speedpilot had two dials. One marked off in divisions from 45 to 130 (irrespective of miles or kilometres), had a hand which could be turned to point to the desired average speed. The other dial had a time clock with a third hand that would be manually positioned behind the hour hand, if the car was driven at faster than the desired average speed the third hand would creep in front of the hour hand, if driven slower than the desired average, it would lag behind. The instrument was controlled by a cable connected to the speedo cable by a 'T' piece at the back of the speedometer.

The Speedpilot was replaced by the Halda Twinmaster, to be used in conjunction with a pair of Heuer clocks. The Twinmaster was a very accurate trip indicator with two displays, one to show overall distance travelled and the other to be tripped between controls or whatever method the navigator favoured.

The Vale of White Horse District Council Highways Division had kindly marked a measured mile and a kilometre on a quiet road through some hop fields near Abingdon. The car would be driven over the distance appropriate to the rally location *i.e.* kilometre when

Anatomy of the Works Minis

The quick-lift jack brackets, painted white for ease of night-time location, under the bumpers.

abroad, or the mile if the event was in the UK. A rev-counter was fixed to the end of the speedo cable to count the number of revolutions that the cable made over the distance. A chart showed which combination of cogs were to be fitted into the Twinmaster to accurately calibrate the instrument.

Even this was not deemed to be foolproof as variations were thought to occur due to

The Hauer clocks seen here alongside the Twinmaster.

Bodyshell and Instruments

The quick-lift jack in action at a pit-stop during the 84 hour Marathon de la Route at Spa. Drivers Tony Fall, Julien Vernaeve, and Andrew Hedges took second place overall.

excessive wheel spin or locking under braking, etc., so another method was tried. Tommy Wellman was given the task of concocting a way of driving the cable from the back wheel. This method was used on the 850 Mini on a Monte Carlo Rally and also on a Cooper S on the Shell 4000 in Canada, where very accurate navigation was called for.

Anatomy of the Works Minis

Speedo drive taken off the rear wheel.

Quick-lift jacks were carried by the service crews and brackets had to be made to provide jacking points. The brackets would be fixed to the front and rear aprons, with their tops hard up under the flange that stands out from the body to carry the bumper. The jack itself was made in the factory's Press Shop.

The Press Shop was once an absolute hive of activity, with heavy presses stamping out the innumerable brackets and plates that went into the building of a motorcar, and the constant flashing of the arc-welders putting together the chassis. But this was before the advent of the MGB with its integral monocoque body/chassis construction being imported to the factory from car body building factories elsewhere. The department was then reduced to making special tools, including the intricate jigs around which the brake and petrol pipes would be bent, to aid the production workers. Other work was undertaken by this department. For a time Riley exhaust manifolds were assembled and welded together for the spare parts store. But gradually this sort of work petered out and the department strength was reduced to a tool maker/turner, Fred Berry, who, incidentally, was the only employee to work in the factory from the time it opened in 1930 until it closed in 1980; Bill Denton, the bench fitter, who was the specialist jig maker for the brake pipes, etc.; Mick Carter, a horizontal grinding machine operator, (who would plane our cylinder heads); and a fitter cum welder cum jack-of-all-trades, Arthur Cookson, who was the man that made our quick-lift racing jacks. This band of skilled men were supervised by their foreman Dick Stevens. Other jobs that they carried out for the Competition Department included making the box trailers that we towed when out servicing rallies, as well as the car transporting trailers and the 'A' frame towbars that could be bolted on to the front of a car allowing it to be towed without a driver.

Because the petrol and brake pipes ran underneath the car, they had to be protected. The ever useful Press Shop boys helped us in this by 'swaging' lengths of mild steel plate to screw over the pipes. These plates were four inches wide when flat and made in three foot lengths. They would be put through rollers, the top roller having a raised semicircular ridge round it and the lower roller having a matching groove. The length of steel was fed in between these rollers which were turned by hand. The result was a length of steel flat down each side and a semicircular channel running down the middle. The flat sides were drilled and screwed to the floor, the channel covering the pipes.

Bodyshell and Instruments

The MG factory Press Shop manufacturing MGA chassis.

The steel Downton exhaust pipe runs close to the car body from the back of the engine and the heat radiated from it was enough to cause the carpet inside the car to smoulder. A half inch thick plate of asbestos measuring a foot by five inches was cut and fixed to the bulkhead to keep the heat at bay. It was found, however, that the asbestos would get soaked as the car drove through deep puddles or streams, causing it to fall apart, so we made an aluminium case to cover it. The carpet in the car also had an asbestos blanket in place of underfelt.

Chapter 3
Subframes and Suspension

The components that make up the subframes are spot-welded together. This is perfectly satisfactory under normal circumstances, but in rally conditions the bits tended to fall apart. This was guarded against by arc-welding all the seams.

Another problem involved the fact that the 'rubber-ball' suspension split the top of the turrets of the front subframe. A false 'cap' had to be made and welded over the original in such a way that it would not arouse the suspicions of a scrutineer.

The brackets that held the 'tie-bars' to keep the front suspension in place were also prone to being broken off, so 'skids' were welded on to deflect rocks, etc. These skids were welded to the bottom of the bracket and to the subframe. Skids were permitted but strengthening brackets were not, so the scrutineer had to be persuaded that they conformed to the letter of the regulations – if not the spirit!

The front shock-absorber brackets were modified to support the outer end of the mounting pin and the self-tapper screws that normally secured the bracket to the wing valance were replaced by $1/4$ UNF bolts screwed into nuts welded to the inside of the valance.

Hydrolastic suspension cars were without separate shock-absorbers until 1968 when an additional front shock absorber kit was developed and homologated. The displacer units were uprated and marked with a blue or double blue band. The pipes that connect the front and rear displacer units were run inside the car for their protection (this called for an intricate piece of pipe-bending on behalf of the fitter).

The rear subframe was, perhaps surprisingly, more prone to breakage than the front one. The frame is basically square. The two longitudinal sides were particularly weak and had to have a 'double skin' welded on to their top length. The wheels

Subframes and Suspension

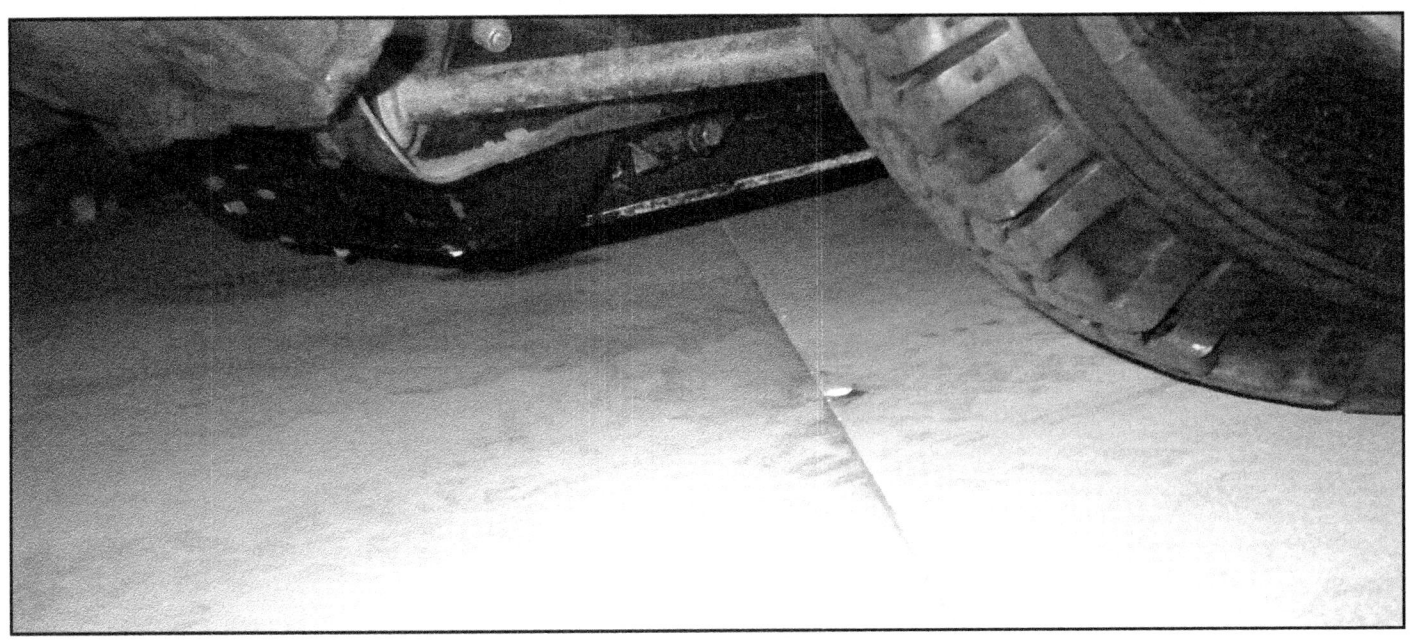

Protection brackets at the front of the tie-bars preventing the bracket from getting ripped off.

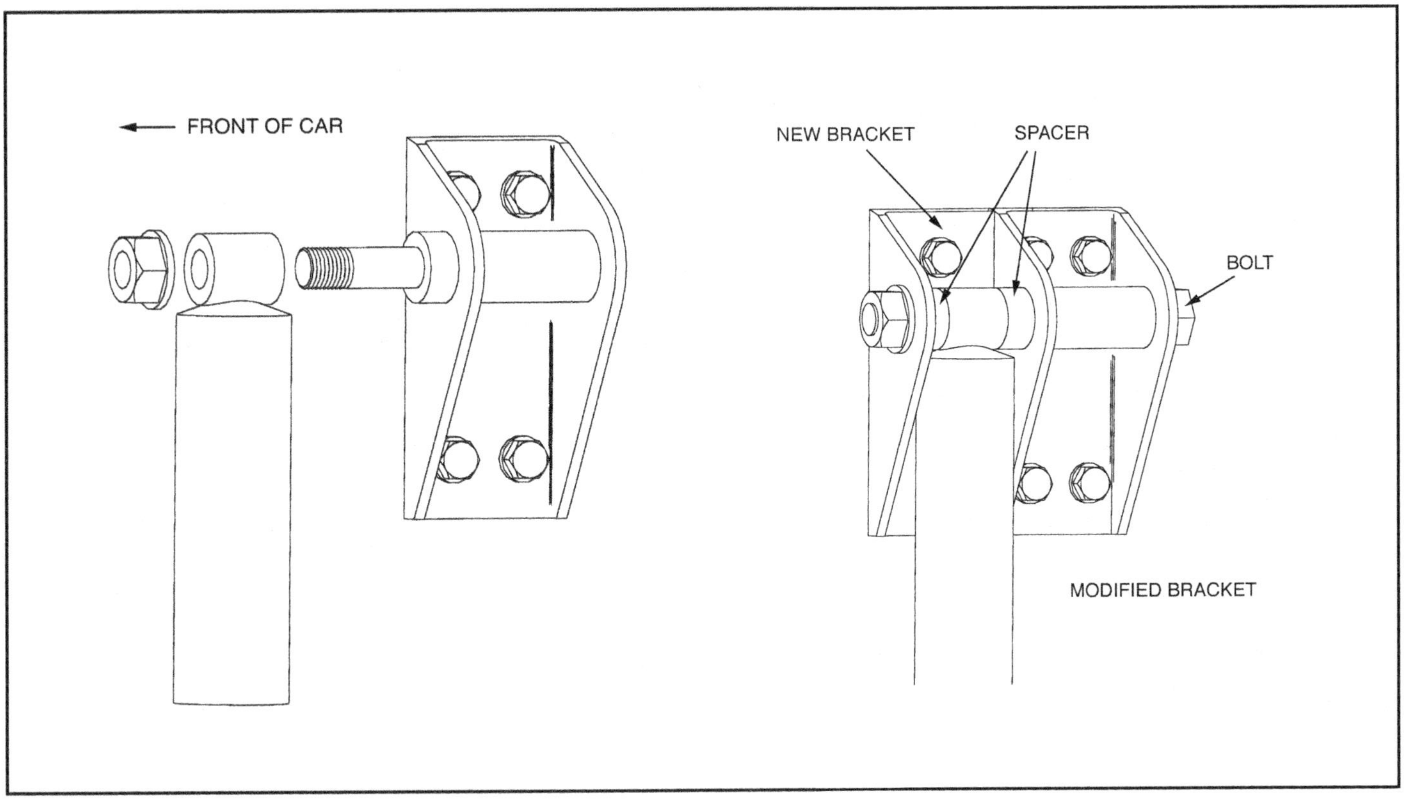

Left: The standard Mini front shock absorber mounting bracket. Right: Drawing showing the shocker mounting modification.

were mounted to the subframe by means of an arm that swiveled where it met the frame. The bracket that secured the arm required strengthening, again by 'double skinning,' that is welding a piece of metal to each surface of the bracket, then carefully filing down the welds to make the fact that the bracket was thicker than normal less obvious. This bracket secured the outer end of the swivel pin. It was bolted into position and no allowance was made for altering the camber angle of the rear wheels.

Initially, it seemed that the geometry of the rear suspension mattered very little since its perceived function was merely to keep the back of the car from dragging along the ground. However, as the car developed and the drivers' appreciation of what was required to get the last ounce of performance from it was sharpened, every small detail was considered. One of these details was the rear suspension geometry, with particular reference to the camber angle, that is the vertical angle that the wheel makes relative to the car.

The production tolerances of all of the contributory elements which governed that angle were sufficient to allow the angle to be different to the one decreed by the designer.

Adjustment was made by slotting the hole in the swivel pin securing bracket. The car would be tested with the pin being tightened at various positions in the slot until the optimum setting was achieved. A washer was then brazed over the slot in the position decided upon, to fix the camber angle permanently.

The battery box is in the floor of the boot and, although it doesn't hang lower than the subframe, it is very vulnerable. Protection for this was made by bolting a plate to the underside of the subframe. The amount of damage that this plate suffered proved its value!

Chapter 4
Footbrakes

'Brake fade' is a common and nasty effect of using the brakes fiercely and often, just as they would have to be used when rushing down a mountain with a hairpin bend every three or four hundred yards. To obviate this condition, a special compound, made by Ferodo, was used in the brake linings. Strangely, this compound would fade once, then, having been faded would give no more trouble. This was one of the jobs that the fitter would do after initial testing and running in of the car. A suitable stretch of road was chosen to drive fast up to high revs in third gear then apply the brakes hard. Before the linings had a chance to cool down the process was repeated until the brakes failed to grip (faded). After a cooling down period the brakes would operate more efficiently than before and not fade again.

Since brake shoes and pads would wear out over the duration of a rally, it was necessary to 'pre-fade' the spares that would be carried by the service crew.

The heat generated by the brakes would boil normal brake fluid, so in the rally cars it was necessary to use a high boiling point fluid, as well as fitting callipers that had asbestos blocks in the pistons to reduce heat transference. On the rear the brake drums and backplates were drilled for extra cooling. The $5/8$" wheel cylinders were bolted directly to the backplates with no gasket, thus further aiding heat transfer.

The brake hoses were protected by a light coil spring over their length. The metal 'Bundy Tubing' pipes that were exposed to the elements were covered with rubber pipe and, where they screwed in to the brake drum or calliper, they were shielded from being sheered off by a specially made protection bracket.

Chapter 5
'Fly-off' Handbrake

To assist in driving round a tight corner quickly the driver would snatch the handbrake on to lock the rear wheels and cause the back end of the car to slide round. The handbrake is normally used as a parking brake and when it is applied a pawl operates on a ratchet preventing the handbrake lever from releasing until a release button in the top of the lever is pressed. When it is being used to assist steering and execute a 'handbrake turn' the lever needs to release as soon as the driver lets go of it. A modification to the pawl was carried out for this purpose. The pawl was made from a short piece of steel 1" (25mm) long by 3/8" (9.5mm) square. One end was curved down like a beaked nose, to catch in the teeth of the ratchet. Halfway along the pawl was a hole that took the pivot pin. At the opposite end to the 'nose' was a vertical slot. A rod coming down from the button at the top of the handbrake lever was riveted into this slot. The button was spring loaded forcing the button up, and with it the back end of the pawl, which swiveled on its central pin thus ensuring that the nose was held down ready to engage in the ratchet when the lever was pulled.

The opposite effect is required to make a 'fly-off' handbrake. The back half of the pawl behind the swivel pin was cut off. This back piece with its slot for the release rod was welded on to the bridge of the nose. Then with the spring holding the button up, it was lifting the nose clear of the ratchet and would only lock into position when the button was depressed. When the handbrake was engaged the tension of the handbrake cables held the pawl into the ratchet, a slight tug on the lever to release that tension allowed the pawl to disengage. After modifying the pawl it had to be case-hardened, as it was before the welding operation, to ensure that the nose would not quickly wear out.

A more sophisticated method of getting quickly round sharp

'Fly-off' Handbrake

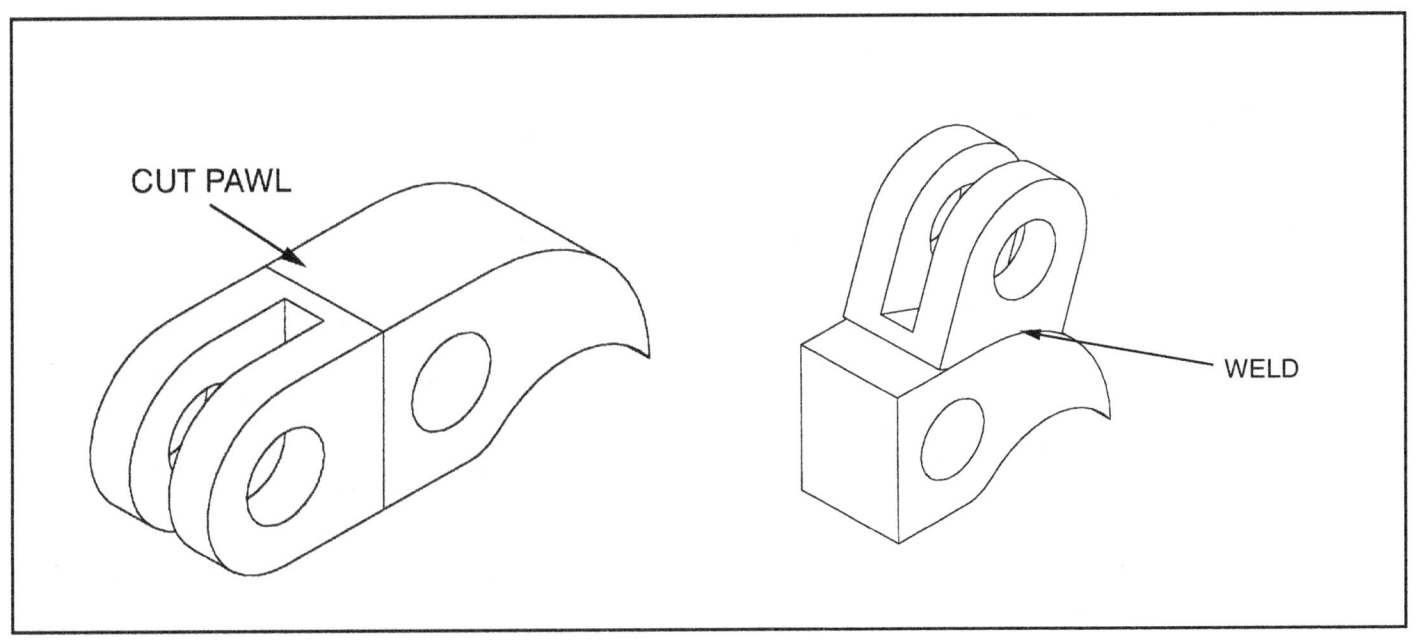

Stages one (left) and two in conversion of handbrake to 'Fly-off' operation.

The accelerator pedal with its extension for ease of 'toe and heel' simultaneous brake and throttle operation.

Anatomy of the Works Minis

bends was devised by the Finns, notably Raunno Aaltonen. This was known as 'left foot braking'. The technique involved using the left foot on the brake pedal and at the same time keeping the right foot hard on the accelerator. This kept the power on, dragging the car through the corner, while the back wheels were locked and skidded round, allowing the driver to keep both hands on the steering wheel and be in complete control.

It is not recommended that this technique is practised on public roads by drivers who have not fully mastered the art.

An instruction in the Build Sheet regarding the accelerator pedal states: modify for toe and heel. The accelerator pedal had a small pad that the driver's foot pressed upon. A metal plate one inch by three inches was welded on to this pad to allow the driver to reach both the brake and the accelerator pedals with one foot, his toe on the brake and his heel on the accelerator. This allowed the driver to brake at the same time as depressing the clutch and revving the engine to select a lower gear.

Chapter 6
Steering

The first instruction on the job sheet under this heading was: "Check the steering column bottom clamp bolt." The need for such a seemingly obvious instruction came about when the column on the Mini being driven by John Sprinzel and Willy Cave on the 1963 Alpine Rally, became disengaged from the steering rack leaving John Sprinzel holding a totally useless steering wheel! The resulting crash into the mountain side, which left the crew with only slight injuries, was better than the plunge over the edge of the road into oblivion which was the only other alternative.

The column was clamped to the steering rack, the clamp bolt

Lucky escape for John Sprinzel/Willy Cave after the steering column came adrift on the 1963 Alpine Rally.

Anatomy of the Works Minis

passed through the clamp and a corresponding locating groove in the steering rack pinion shaft. The clamp bolt on this occasion was through the column clamp, but not the locating groove. The bolt was tightened in an incorrect position, which was sufficient to hold the column into position until a tug on the steering wheel pulled it apart from the rack.

The next instruction on the build sheet was: "Fit modified U-bolt to location side of steering rack." The fierce and constant changes of direction caused the rack to move and eventually work loose. The rack is held in place by two U-bolts. The one at the pinion end locates in a channel cast into the rack's body. This channel is very slightly wider than the U-bolt and no matter how much the U-bolt was tightened the rack would move from side to side, very slightly to start with, but increasing as the movement wore the U-bolt down. The modification was to run a bead of weld round the edge of the U-bolt then file it down to make it a perfect fit in its channel, thus preventing the rack from loosening.

"Shim Rack to .003" [inch]." The steering rack is more properly referred to as the rack and pinion. The pinion is a toothed gear that is turned by the steering column. The rack is the bar that is moved from side to side by teeth cut in it to mesh with the pinion. The steering rack would be stripped down and carefully reassembled. The toothed rack had to mesh deeply into the teeth of the pinion, held firmly in mesh by a spring loaded pad. Shims had to be fitted to ensure that the spring could only compress by three thousandths of an inch.

"Steering arms – lap faces." The steering arms are bolted to the swivel hub. These arms would inexplicably work loose. Advice was sought from the design office who came up with the theory that although the face of the swivel hub was smooth, the face of the steering arm was roughly machined and, despite being carefully tightened and dowelled into position, the arm would find itself some movement and work to wear away the ridges on the face of the arm. Our task, then, was to smooth the face of the arm and, with carborundum paste, lap it to the swivel hub face. A laborious and time-consuming job.

Chapter 7
Wheels

The magnesium alloy Minilite wheels were not homologated for use on the Mini until the Monte Carlo rally of 1967. Prior to this the cars ran on the standard 4½" wide 10" diameter steel wheels, though fitted with a variety of tyres chosen by the racers and a multitude of different mud and snow tyres for appropriate events.

In the early days of Mini racing the centre ripped out of the steel wheel. The manufacturers were quickly alerted because the problem caused the Mini to be banned from all RAC competitions. When the strengthened wheels were made available they were brought to Abingdon and stamped with an MG logo. Only cars with wheels

Minilite wheels as used on the 1970 World Cup Rally.

Anatomy of the Works Minis

Centre locked Minilite wheel.

Below: Centre locked wheel in situ.

carrying this stamp were allowed by the RAC scrutineers until the new wheels were standard fitting.

The Minilite wheel was a much stronger wheel than the original, and had the added advantage of being lighter too. Magnesium wheels of the Minilite type were used on all Works cars from 1967 on.

The 12" diameter wheel developed for the Cooper racing team was rarely used on rally cars because the high tyre temperatures generated by constant high speed cornering on tarmac was not so prevalent under rally conditions and the different handling characteristics

Wheels

Spanners to secure the centre locked wheels.

were not to the rally drivers' liking.

In 1969 a centre locking Minilite wheel was designed. A flanged hub was bolted on to the wheel studs and the wheel was fixed to this by an octagonal nut and a special spanner was made to fit. This system was never used on an event but a centre lock wheel with a 'knock-on' spinner type nut was used on the Mini that John Handley drove on the 1969 Tour de France.

Anatomy of the Works Minis

Centre locked wheel with knock-on type fixing as used on the 1969 Tour de France.

Chapter 8
Engine

Even in the mildly tuned form permitted under Group 2 regulations there was a lot of work to be done to the engine. The cylinder block was bored out to +.020" to increase the cubic capacity of the engine.

The crankshaft and pistons would be temporarily fitted and a measurement taken to ascertain the amount of space between the top of the cylinder block and the piston when the latter was at the top of its stroke. The depth of this space was required to be .010". The standard production figure was greater than this and not constant, therefore, the amount to be machined off the top face differed from block to block. It was important that this figure was correct to give the desired compression ratio.

Another part of the calculation was the size of the combustion space in the cylinder head. The combustion chamber was polished where regulations permitted, and the amount of metal polished out had to leave each of the four chambers with exactly equal capacity. Having achieved this it was then necessary to measure the displacement. The specification on the engine for the 1966 German Rally car driven by Tony Fall called for a compression ratio of 12.6:1.

A calculation based on the capacity of the cylinder divided by the total combustion space showed that, with the space at the top of the piston known, plus the thickness of the gasket, the space in the cylinder head should be 16.4 cubic centimetres.

It was calculated that shaving .012" from the face of the cylinder head would reduce the combustion space by one cubic centimetre. Having arrived at a figure it was over to the Press Shop with the cylinder block and head for Mick Carter, the machinist, to grind the required amount from each of them.

Great importance was placed on balancing the engine in every way, the attention paid to the

43

Anatomy of the Works Minis

BMC mechanic Bob Whittington balancing con-rods.

size of combustion spaces was one important aspect of this, another was the strength of the valve springs and each one had to be individually checked before fitting.

The weight of each reciprocating part also had to be equal. The connecting rods, for example, had to weigh the same (not just overall, but the four big ends had to be the same weight, as had the four small ends – and the lighter the better). When an event permitted it, the rods were weighed and ground to the same weight. Grinding and filing leaves grooves in the surface of the metal, each of which is a potential fracture point. Therefore, after balancing, the rods would have to be polished to leave a smooth surface. The standard rod had a rough but not grooved finish so had no potential fracture points.

On an event where polishing of engine components was not allowed it was necessary to take a bin full of con-rods and weigh them to find a matching set. The first fitter to get to that stage of building the engine selected the best matched and lightest set. It was not unusual that a fitter, down the selecting order,

couldn't find an acceptable set of rods. In this case Neville Challis, the stores foreman, would have to restock and send the odd ones back to production where their effect would be lost among the other items made to within production tolerances to provide an acceptable standard engine. It was unlikely, but not impossible of course, that all the items at the top of the production tolerances came together to make an exceptionally good engine. At the other end of the scale, however, the reverse could be true.

Before fitting the piston to the con-rod, an additional oil hole was drilled in the gudgeon pin boss to allow for better lubrication. With the piston fitted, the con-rod had to be lined up on a precision made tool which had a bar representing the crankshaft journal, and a plate at a right-angle to the bar. The big-end of the con-rod was bolted to the bar and the piston was laid against the plate. The skirt of the piston was larger in diameter than the top (head).

Feeler gauges would measure the gap between the piston head and the plate. The assembly would be removed, turned around and the same measurement taken. Any discrepancy was remedied by using a special clamp on the con-rod to bend it!

There was no facility for balancing the crankshaft in the factory. Therefore, the crank/flywheel/clutch assembly (with its specially reinforced diaphragm to eliminate clutch slip) had to sent to the engineering firm of Hunts of Poole, in Dorset, to be lightened and balanced.

The cylindrical cam-followers were bored out to leave the walls thinner and lighter. The camshaft sprocket was pierced with lightening holes. The sprocket is the gear on the front of the camshaft and is chain driven off a gear on the crankshaft. The chain has to run absolutely straight and true.

On the standard engine the crankshaft sprocket sits slightly further back on its shaft than does the one on the camshaft. This means that thin shims have to be fitted behind the crankshaft sprocket to bring it into line with its fellow on the camshaft.

It had been found that the crankshaft sprocket had a tendency to work loose. This was put down to the fact that the pounding of the crank against the sprocket was destroying the shims. The sprocket and the fanbelt pulley had been bolted tight against the shims, and their destruction was the cause of the problem. The sprockets, then, had to be aligned without the use of shims. A straight-edge laid across the face of the teeth of both sprockets showed how far they were misaligned. Normally this would be corrected by the shims, bringing the crankshaft sprocket forward, but now the result would be achieved by having the appropriate amount machined off the back of the camshaft sprocket.

The rocker gear also came in for a lot of modification (again,

Anatomy of the Works Minis

Engine tuning ace Cliff Humphreys assembling a Mini engine.

where permitted). The rockers are the levers that the pushrods from the camshaft act upon to open the valves. It had been found that removing .055" from the height of the pillars which carried the rockers brought about greater opening of the valves.

The rockers themselves were drastically lightened and polished too, with the pad that acted on the valve being narrowed to the same width as the diameter of the valve stem. For standard engines the rockers were spaced on a shaft with a light spring between them to keep them in place. However, the amount of movement allowed by the spring could mean that the narrowed rocker might not sit squarely on the end of the valve. Also, the springs acting on the side of the rockers were a source of unnecessary friction. These springs were replaced by steel spacers, which we dubbed 'cotton reels' because of their shape. They were made by Fred Berry and were fitted over the shaft between each rocker.

The shaft carrying the rockers was supported by four pillars. Rockers number one and eight were on the ends of the shaft beyond the last supporting pillar. The pillar by number one rocker was drilled to allow oil to pass through it. The shaft was hollow to allow oil to be fed to the rockers, it

Engine

had an oil-hole which lined up with the hole in the pillar. In order that this hole remained in its correct position there was another hole to accept a dowel screw. So the end of the shaft, where it passed through the pillar, had two holes in it. On one event the shaft broke across these two holes causing serious damage to the engine. To overcome this problem, a shaft was produced that had the dowel hole positioned where it passed through the second pillar, which itself had to be modified to accept the dowel screw. This shaft, then, with only the oil hole at the vulnerable end, was much stronger.

With all of the components modified as instructed and the machining carried out on the head and the block, it was vital to clean out any vestige of the metal grindings that would have inevitably found their way into the oil-galleries. One of the great deficiencies of the workshop equipment was the lack of a proper cleaning bath.

All cleaning was carried out in a tin tray with paraffin and a brush then a squirt through the oilways with a syringe, followed by flushing through all the galleries and nooks and crannies, with the high-pressure water hose of the factory car-wash! Finally, after drying and flushing through again with oil, the engine would be rebuilt.

An entry in the Build Sheet regarding the big-end bolts stated: "Stretch big-end bolts to .003"." Great attention was paid to this instruction after a big-end bolt broke on Raymond Baxter's 1965 Monte Carlo Rally Mini in far away Minsk, Russia.

The bolts were measured with a micrometer before tightening to the recommended torque figure then measured again. Bolts stretch when tightened and will resume their original length when loosened if they have not been stretched beyond their 'elastic limit.' The torque setting is calculated to stretch the bolt to that limit, which, in the case of the Mini big-end bolt is .003", any more and the bolt would be discarded.

The gaskets on all the plates and covers that needed to be oil-leak free were smeared with a blue glue-like sealant called Hylomar (recommended for use on Rolls-Royce engines). It was important not to overdo the use of this because any sealant that squeezed out into the engine would roll itself into little balls resulting in the danger of it clogging the oilways. It was an excellent sealant, however, and had the added virtue of remaining pliable and would clean off easily when the engine was next stripped.

On the Group 2 engine it was permissible to change the inlet manifold and fit 1½ inch carburettors. They were bigger in every way than the standard Mini carbs and needed a manifold that would incline them upwards away from the bulkhead crossmember, but this resulted in the float chamber being at an undesirable

Anatomy of the Works Minis

angle. This problem was corrected by heating the stem that connects the float chamber to the main carb and twisting it. The result was that the float chamber was level, but too low to achieve the correct fuel level in the jet. As the fuel level cut-off valve was part of the float chamber top, an extension piece was made to raise the float chamber top by $1/2$ an inch.

The fan belts were specially checked before leaving the Mintex factory following a rather dubious occurrence on the Tour of Corsica. The cars used on that event were fitted with special fuel injected engines and had undergone extensive testing. Imagine the disbelief when, on the first of the night-time stages, the engines overheated and the lights dimmed on both of the cars. The fanbelts were found to be loose. Although mechanics were on hand to adjust the belts, they were soon slipping again and both cars retired with overheated engines and flat batteries. The fault was diplomatically attributed to a bad batch of fanbelts but, although the cars were locked in a supposedly secure park on the night before the event, sabotage was not ruled out …

Chapter 9
Gearbox

The helical gears in a normal gearbox have the teeth on the gearwheels cut diagonally to achieve a low noise level. However, gears cut in this manner are not as strong as those that are cut straight across, 'spur gears.' These spur gears gave a distinctive whine and provided adequate warning of the approach of a Works Mini to a service point on a rally. This whine gave rise to the parody on *Hark the Herald Angels Sing*, written for a Competition Department Christmas party:

Hark the Mini gearbox sings, Raunno Aaltonen it brings, to our humble Service Point, Contemplating his Birfield joint, backwards round the corner skating, left foot braking demonstrating, keep the ham and chicken hidden, from his navigator Liddon, don't let him know how much we've got, or he will scoff the bloody lot!

Henry Liddon, was a big man with a big appetite and a liking for the tins of chicken supreme that we carried. It was part of the mechanic's job to provide refreshments at service points for the crews and Henry's appetite was a standing joke. He was a very popular member of the team and his death in an aeroplane accident years later, after the BMC Competition Department had been closed, was deeply mourned.

The gearbox, then, was completely stripped and the case taken over to the Press Shop to have the bottom of it machined flat. This was to allow for the fitting of the 'Moke Type' sump shield, which was a 3/16" thick steel plate screwed on to the bottom of the box with the front bent up to provide added protection.

The new gears were close ratio gears, this meant that first second and third gears were all higher ratios than standard and lessened the difference between third and top gear. Internal combustion engines only operate

Anatomy of the Works Minis

The straight-cut gears, stronger than the standard helical gears.

at maximum efficiency over a narrow band of revolutions. Normally, when changing gear from third to top the engine's speed drops below its band of maximum efficiency causing slower acceleration at high speeds. The close ratio gears are designed to eliminate this problem. Of course you don't get something for nothing and the higher first gear meant sacrificing some acceleration speed from a standing start. However, for competition use this is seen as the lesser of the two evils.

When rebuilding the gearbox the first items to go in were the selector rods with their forks. These were right in the bottom of the gearbox and were inaccessible after the rest of the fittings were in place. The savage gearchanging, often without recourse to the clutch, could loosen the small securing screws, so a 'belt and braces' job was done on the screws and their locknuts. As well as being coated with Loctite and carefully tightened, they were drilled and wire-locked.

The oil pick-up pipe was modified to pick up the oil from the centre of the gearbox instead of from one side. This was to overcome the effects of oil surge on corners.

Chapter 10
Electrics

The extra electrical equipment fitted to a rally car put a great strain on the circuitry and the dynamo (which was soon superseded by the stronger alternator). The high engine speeds of the rally car caused the alternator to run too fast, however, and a large diameter pulley was fitted to overcome this problem. Changing a fanbelt on a Mini is not an easy or quick job due to the fan running close to the radiator cowl. The precaution was taken of clipping a spare belt behind the pulleys, ready to effect a quick change if required at a service point on a rally.

The standard wiring harness was discarded, to be replaced by the one that was custom-made by the Lucas technicians working with the fitter who was preparing the car. Initially, with perhaps six cars to prepare, all of the measurements would be taken and six harnesses made to the same pattern. The cable used was of the linen covered variety instead of the plastic covered, but the colour coding was kept the same for all of the standard fittings. The cable was kept on reels mounted on a stand. Having cut all of the cables to the required lengths they were expertly bound together with tape, the finished object resembling a grape vine with branches sprouting out at precisely the right place to connect with the appropriate appliance, switch, or lamp. This was a very complex task due to so much of the electrical equipment being non-standard.

The headlights, fitted with iodine bulbs, were 60 watts on main beam and 40 watts on dip. This high wattage meant that each lamp on high beam was taking 5 amps which was too high a load to be carried by the headlamp switch. The switch, therefore, was used to operate a relay which carried the higher amperage to the lamp. Each beam was fed by its individual relay. Another cause of extra

Anatomy of the Works Minis

wiring for the headlamps was the addition of a flasher switch (non-standard in early Mini days).

There were also two fog and two long range lamps, each with a separate switch and relay. These lamps were mounted on a bar that stretched across the front of the car, and were connected via a multiplug facilitating the quick removal of the lamp assembly if repairs were needed to the front of the engine, for example. It was also convenient for removing the lamps during daylight hours to save weight and remove the risk of damage.

High decibel air-operated horns replaced the normal ones, and these too were operated by a relay. In addition to the horn button for the driver's use, a foot-operated horn button was provided for the navigator. When driving flat out round blind mountain bends, using all of the road which might or might not be closed to other traffic, the navigator's foot would be hard down on the button from one side of the mountain to the other.

A two-speed wiper motor replaced the original single speed model. A switch was provided for both the driver and navigator. The wiper blades were operated by a flexible steel wire rack, fixed off-centre to a wheel in the motor. As the wheel rotated the rack passed from side to side across toothed wheels that carried the wiper arms. These wheels were made of a fibrous material and the constant labour of keeping the screen clear of snow stripped the teeth from them. Special wheelboxes were designed to overcome this. Normally, the teeth protruded from the edge of the driving wheel, engaging with the teeth of the rack which ran across the top. The modified wheelbox contained a wheel of a similar thickness to the diameter of the rack. A concave channel was cut around the rim of the wheel and the teeth formed in this channel. The result was that the rack had half of its circumference in contact with the wheel, instead of just one edge as before.

Tony Fall looking pleased to find that the lamp bar can be removed to give access to the front of the engine.

Electrics

The fitter's role in all this was to mount the switches into the instrument panels that Stan Bradford, the shop's panel beater, had made; make up brackets to carry the relays and extra fuse boxes; make holes through the bulkheads to allow the new harnesses to pass through; and generally be at the electrician's bidding. There was no drawing to adhere to that laid down precisely where the extra items were to be fitted and the cables were not cut until the electrician came to actually make the connections. This was just another instance of how each car's preparation differed from the others.

The battery was turned round for reasons that will be described in the next chapter.

The starter switch, incorporated with the ignition switch, had failed to operate on a couple of occasions in the past, so a separate starter button was wired in to ensure that this didn't happen again.

John Smith, Lucas technician carrying out complete re-wiring.

An electric windscreen washer replaced the old syphon squirter and the plastic washer jets were discarded in favour of chrome-plated ones. These were preferred because they were stronger and gave a better jet. The chrome plating was incidental, of course, and the jets, along with the chrome wiper arms and anything else that might disturb the driver's night vision, were painted matt black.

The only luxury item fitted to the rally Mini was a cigar lighter (two, in fact, one each for the driver and navigator!)

Anatomy of the Works Minis

The long stalk of the Headlamp Flasher switch.

Electrics

The ultimate Monte Carlo Rally Mini with multi-pin wired detachable lamp bar, heated windscreen, Minilite wheels, etc. Driven by Paddy Hopkirk to 5th place in 1968.

Chapter 11
Fuel System

The standard fuel tank on the left hand side of the car was augmented by the addition of one on the right. It was this tank that got smashed out of position when Raunno Aaltonen, driving in his first Monte for BMC, hit an outcrop of rock. The crash drove the tank against the battery terminals causing a massive short circuit and starting a fire that gutted the car (Raunno was lucky to escape with his life). From that time the rally cars had their batteries turned around to take the terminals away from the tank.

The way the tank was fastened was also modified by moving

The petrol tank strap round the outside of the flange.

Fuel System

The petrol tank strap inboard of the flange on the 1970 World Cup Rally Mini.

Raunno Aaltonen's burnt out Mini. The result of the petrol tank being smashed against the battery.

Anatomy of the Works Minis

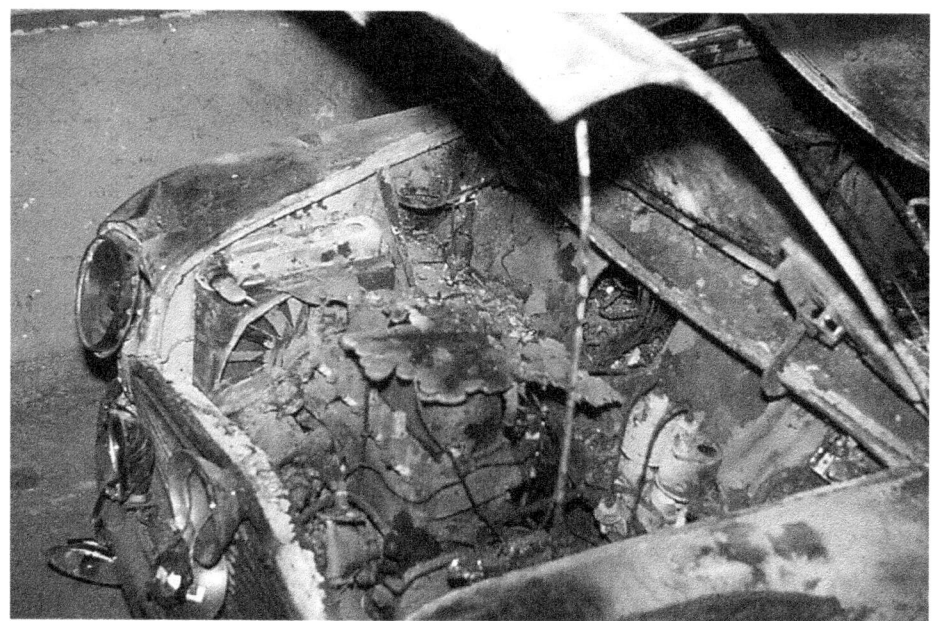

The melted carburettors.

The interior from where Geoff Mabbs dragged the unconscious Raunno Aaltonen.

the fixing strap inboard of the flange round the tank. A sheet of asbestos was stuck to the tank as a further protection. On any event where studded tyres were used, the asbestos sheet was replaced by plywood to protect the tank from the sharp studs of the spare wheels that were carried in the boot.

As described earlier, the fuel pipes were either run inside the car or protected by a metal channel under the car. The two fuel pumps were electric and, when possible, were mounted under the rear seat with only one pump wired: the other was a standby unit.

The filler caps were wired or chained to the filler neck to prevent them from being dropped during rapid refuelling.

Chapter 12
Miscellaneous

With the engine and gearbox built and bolted together there were a great many minor jobs to be done before the car was ready. The dipstick, for example, was heated at the end until it turned blue (this made the oil level easier to see than it was against the plain metal dipstick).

The special yellow high tension leads to the spark plugs were liberally smeared with silicon grease before being fixed into the distributor cap; this to keep out any moisture that found its way through the rubber glove-like cover. The centre post in the distributor itself was given a light smear of grease to help lengthen the life of the contact breaker. Despite this, however, the fibre heel of the contact breaker sustains a lot of initial wear and, after a period of running the points would have to be adjusted for they would have closed up slightly. If this was not attended to after a hundred miles, or so, the wear could be enough to allow the points to close up sufficiently to prevent the engine from starting. An early sign of this was the engine stalling when running slowly.

The electrically operated temperature gauge was discarded in favour of the older capillary type which had a bulb that was screwed into the cylinder head and an armoured capillary tube that went to the gauge. The bulb and the tube contained ether which reacted to the heat and operated the gauge.

Part of the engine's closed circuit breather system was referred to as the 'clack valve.' This was connected to the inlet manifold by a short hose. The object of the system was to reduce air pollution by feeding the oil vapour from the crankcase back into the engine. This was liable to upset the fuel mixture, however, and have a detrimental effect on the engine efficiency. The clack valve was part of the engine ancillary equipment that had to remain in place to conform to the regulations, but it was

Anatomy of the Works Minis

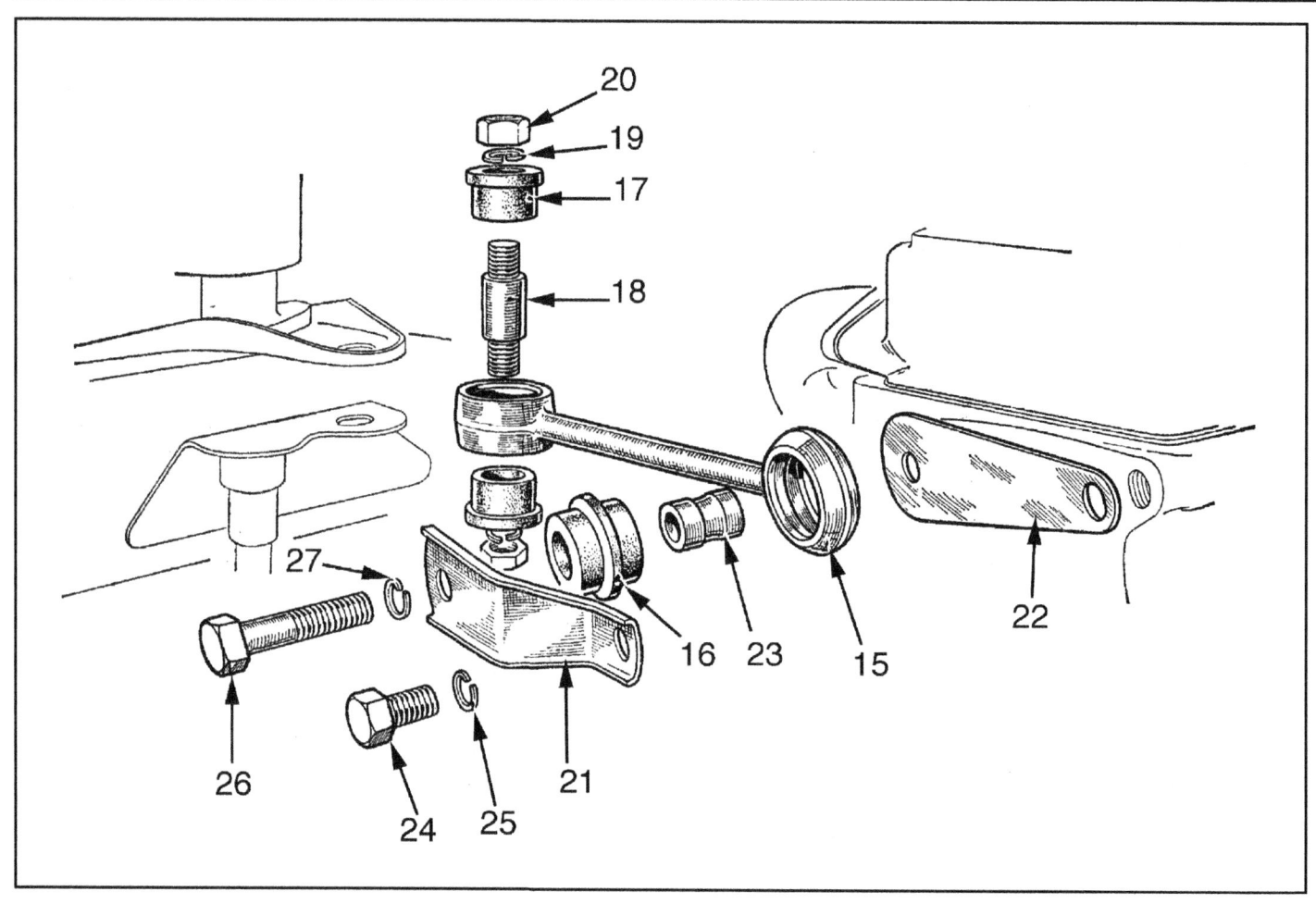

Item 18 replaced by a nut and bolt.

made inoperative and a hole was cut in the hose to allow the pressure to be released to the atmosphere. The oil filler cap was also drilled to relieve the pressure from inside the rocker cover.

The engine steady bar that restricted the torque movement of the engine, went from the engine to the bulkhead. The bulkhead end of the bar was secured by a bolt made from a short piece of bar with a thread sticking out of either end. This bolt was placed into a bracket welded to the bulkhead, then the rubber bush and steady bar dropped on to it with another bracket on top to make a sandwich of the steady bar. This upper bracket was fixed by the same bolts that secured the master cylinders, so it was not possible to remove the steady bar or the fixing bolt without first removing the master cylinders. Unfortunately, the rubber bush came in for a lot of punishment due to the fierce braking and acceleration in competition, causing the engine to lurch back and forth, and frequently had to be replaced. The solution that was adopted was to do away with the fixing bolt with its thread at either end and replace it with a straightforward bolt and nut with a spacer in the rubber bush.

The gearbox remote control mounting was a straightforward round rubber, 2 inch in diameter, with a plate with a threaded stud protruding from its centre bonded on to one side, and

Miscellaneous

The mounting rubber at the rear of the remote gear change was modified by Terry Mitchell.

another plate with two fixing holes bonded to the other. The distance of this mounting from the centre of the engine mountings, however, magnified all of the engine movement and the rubber was ripped apart. A modification to the mounting was designed by Terry Mitchell. The stud that protruded from one side was extended into the rubber with a ball on the inner end. The stud passed through a cup fixed to the plate of the other side. The two sides couldn't then part company. The cup was perforated and the whole assembly bonded with rubber, making it almost indistinguishable from the original. The engine still exerted the same amount of force, though, and, because the mounting rubber wouldn't break, it now broke the mounting bracket away from where it was fixed to the body under the gearbox tunnel in between the seats. This resulted in the need for more judicious body strengthening.

The exhaust system was designed and manufactured by Downtons. It was made in three pieces, the downpipe from the engine fitted into the pipe which ran to the silencer at the back of

Anatomy of the Works Minis

the car. Where the pipes joined, in addition to the standard clamp, lugs were welded onto adjoining pipes and a strap was bolted across the join, ensuring that no amount of buffeting would knock the system apart.

The rubber mountings of the exhaust system had a short life due to the punishment that the system endured and so they were modified by cutting off the stud that the exhaust bracket bolted to, then drilling straight through the rubber and fitting a bolt for the bracket to screw to. The bracket was secured to the bolt with a Nylock nut and this arrangement allowed the rubber to have some movement but not to tear apart.

The front of the silencer was particularly vulnerable so, to protect it, we welded a length of steel plate from the bottom edge of the silencer up to the pipe forming a slide to shield it from direct hits.

Chapter 13
The Moment of Truth

With the car finally completed, it was time to fill the engine with oil and water. This, unfortunately, was taken literally by one apprentice. The Mini engine is filled with oil through a filler in the top of the rocker cover, it takes time for the oil to find its way down into the gearbox and, if one isn't careful, the rocker cover can fill up and overflow. The apprentice was told to "fill the engine and mind it doesn't overflow." He did just that, carefully filling the engine right up to the top of the filler cap causing the fitter great consternation when black oil smoke billowed out of the exhaust when the engine was started. It was soon cured when it was realised what had happened and the oil was drained to the correct level. But the apprentice never lived it down ...

Filled with oil and water, and with some petrol in the tank, the ignition was switched on for the first time (with a hasty check round for fuel leaks or flooding from a sticky or wrongly adjusted carburettor float needle).

Then the starter button was pressed and, all being well, your painstakingly assembled engine burst into life. More checking for leaks, then the bonnet was fitted and the car driven out of the factory on its maiden run. After half an hour driving round the Oxfordshire countryside listening for knocks and rattles it was back to the workshop and straight up onto the high-lift for a thorough inspection.

All being well, the car then underwent a 300 mile running-in period. This was carried out in the fitter's own time during evenings or weekends when he was allowed to use the car as he wished, so long as the miles were put on.

After this time the cylinder head nuts were retightened to the correct torque setting, the tappets and contact breakers readjusted and the car handed over to Cliff Humphries. Cliff's job was to fine tune the engine

Anatomy of the Works Minis

Paddy Hopkirk inspecting his finished rally car. Note the headlamp washer on the stalk.

on the rolling road and coax the maximum torque and power from it.

It was then the fitter's job to see if the acceleration and top speed figures lived up to the rolling road results. There were various quiet roads in the area where this testing could take place. They needed to be flat and fairly straight with no road junctions. The acceleration figure that we were particularly interested in was 0-60mph. This needed a clean, quick start, foot flat on the floor up to 6000rpm, then a quick gear change to second then third. A partner in the passenger seat timed these runs using a stopwatch. Timings were taken in both directions along the road, and the top speed was recorded. The accelerator pedal had to held hard down in top gear, until the rev counter maintained a maximum reading of 6800rpm or more, depending on the stage of tune of the engine.

When the car was tuned and finished to the fitter's satisfaction it was given to Eddie Burnell for final testing. Eddie was a highly skilled fitter and capable of driving a rally or race car as fast and as punishingly as the works drivers. The fitter accompanied Eddie on the test run and was treated to a breathtaking ride, making him acutely aware of the importance of every nut and bolt that he had used. Eddie's route used the open, sometimes tortuous roads of the Berkshire Downs, where the tanks built in the factory during the war were taken for testing. He seemed able to hear, feel, or sense every weakness. Back in the workshop he would make out a list of rattles, squeaks, or other imperfections that in his opinion needed attention. Sometimes his robust handling of the car showed up a weakness that the fitter needed convincing really existed. But if Eddie said there was, for instance, a suspect bearing in the gearbox, then out it had to come and the cause investigated.

With the car fully run in and finished it would be put back on the rolling-road dynamometer for Cliff Humphreys to produce a test sheet showing the power figures, etc.

Finally, there was the visit of the driver and navigator. Invariably the seats needed adjusting, whether forward, back, sideways or up and down. Pedals needed to be further apart or closer together. The steering wheel position often needed to be adjusted. Another electric socket might be required to suit the latest gadget that the navigator had found.

When everything was finally carried out to everyone's satisfaction, the car was taken to the factory's paint shop once more for touching up and polishing. Once the car took its place at rally scrutineering, the critical eyes of the scrutineering inspectors and

The Moment of Truth

the world's motoring press would pass judgement on the finish of the motor car, just as harshly as the performance in the rally would show how efficient had been your preparation.

Between 1962 and 1968 the Mini's international rally results were: 27 outright wins, 10 second places and 9 thirds.

Appendix A
The Racing Mini
(With information supplied by Ginger Devlin, Cooper's Chief Mechanic)

Suspension modifications on a Mini racer

The excellent handling abilities of the Mini encouraged Alec Issigonis to consider the possibility of enhanced prestige to be gained on the race track. John Cooper, who ran one of the more successful racing teams of that time, proved to be enthusiastic too. In 1961, then, as a result of this collaboration, the Mini Cooper, fitted with the 997cc Mini engine based on that of the Formula Junior, came into being.

At first the suspension modifications were quite limited, with just stiffer shock absorbers being fitted. The front suspension trumpets were shortened by $3/8$" to lower the front of the car by about 1" - $1^1/4$". The flange of the trumpet was reduced in diameter, this had the effect of compressing less of the suspension rubber giving a softer ride and lessening the tendency to understeer. The reverse was used on the rear, with van type trumpets being used which had a larger flange thereby compressing more rubber and stiffening the rear suspension. This trumpet was also shortened by $3/8$."

All of the suspension mounting rubbers were replaced by a heavier duty rubber compound and the top suspension arm was modified to reduce its length and give some negative camber. The front bump rubbers were shortened to delay their contact with the bump stop so as to further reduce understeer.

The rear radius arm outer fixing bracket was altered to give $1/4$ of a degree of negative camber as opposed to the 1 degree positive standard setting. A high ratio steering rack was also fitted.

Standard wheels were used with normal road pattern tyres (C41s), moulded in racing rubber.

As the cars progressed from 997cc to the 1071cc and 1275cc

Anatomy of the Works Minis

Ginger Devlin in front of John Rhodes' Mini Cooper at Brands Hatch.

Cooper S, so wider and wider wheels were used, culminating with 8" on the front and 6" on the rear. These were now magnesium alloy, replacing the standard pressed steel versions.

A rear anti-roll bar was introduced to promote some oversteer going into corners and combat the understeer on the way out. This anti-roll bar was mounted at the rear of the subframe with arms going forward to be connected by short links to the radius arms.

The bottom arm, or 'track-control arm', on the front suspension was modified with an adjustable rose joint at the inner end so that the negative camber could be adjusted to even out the tyre temperature across the wider tyres. This adjustment was made according to the type of circuit. At Brands Hatch, for example, as much as 3 degrees of negative camber was used on the outer front with one degree on the inner, due to most of the tighter corners on the small circuit being

The Racing Mini

right-handed, especially the first one after the start ('Paddock'), followed by the 'Druids' hairpin.

Before the start of the 1965 season the motorsports governing body, the FIA in Paris, announced a regulation stating that the entire wheel and tyre should be within the mudguard. However, with negative camber the bottom of the Mini wheel was outside the vertical line from the edge of the mudguard to the ground. Even a standard Mini didn't comply with this regulation, so a meeting was hastily convened by the RAC between Henry Taylor (the Ford Competition Manager), Stuart Turner of BMC, a representative from the Rootes group and from Standard Triumph, plus Ginger Devlin representing the Cooper Car Company. The meeting was chaired by Dean Delamont from the RAC, with Stuart Proctor the RAC scrutineer for Group 2 lending his advice. Ginger put forward the suggestion that a small wing extension made from fibreglass could be marketed if it was acceptable as a means of bringing the car into compliance.

The scheme was presented to the FIA and was accepted, provided that it did not increase the overall width of the car by more than 5cm a side. The widest part of a Mini is at the 'B pillar', behind the driver's door, which is 8cm a side wider than the front wing. This easily allowed the wing extension to be large enough to cover the whole wheel. Thus the 'eyebrows' seen on the Mini wings as a fashion accessory, were actually born of necessity.

The arrival of hydrolastic suspension added a new set of problems. BMC insisted that hydrolastic suspension should be presented to the public as an improvement. The first problem to show itself, however, was the increase in understeer. As the car accelerated the back settled down squashing the fluid forward and raising the front end. This reduced the negative camber causing less of the tyre to be in contact with the road. Special shock absorbers were tried to cure the problem, but eventually taps were put into the fluid pipes to lock off the transfer of fluid from front to rear. There was some question as to whether or not this mod complied with the Group 2 regulations. Approval was given, however, as it was deemed to be a modification to the shock-absorber which, on the hydrolastic suspension, is integral with the displacer unit (and besides, Ralph Broad of Broadspeed, Cooper's rival on the race tracks, was already using it). The car with its modified hydrolastic suspension proved to be superior to the dry suspension in wet conditions due to the reduction of wheel 'patter', allowing the wheel to be in more constant contact with the road and reducing further the tendency to understeer.

The Mini racing engine
The cars were being raced under Group 2 regulations which limited

Anatomy of the Works Minis

Wing extensions, a Ginger Devlin innovation.

the amount of modification that could take place. The camshaft was changed and the 1¼" SU carburettors replaced by 1½" SUs.

High compression pistons were fitted to give 11:1 compression ratio and the inlet and exhaust ports were reshaped and polished to give better fuel flow.

A close ratio gearbox was used as on the rally cars. The final drive ratio was changed according to the circuit on which a race was to take place.

These engines were produced in the Development Department of the Morris engine plant in Coventry under the supervision of Eddie Maher. The Development Department had the pressures of developing for production and Cooper didn't feel that the new 1275cc engine was achieving its potential. This suspicion was heightened when Cliff Humphreys at the BMC Competitions Department at Abingdon suggested that they should try one of the Competition engines which was fitted with a Downton

cylinder head. The improvement was sufficient for Cooper to form an association with Danny Richmond of Downton, which lasted until the Cooper team was disbanded in 1969.

Cooper had changed from using the SU carburettors to the 45DCOE Weber carbs which, although giving only marginal improvement at the top end of the rev range, gave a hefty 12 extra horse power around 5800-6000rpm. Downton, meanwhile, had produced a modified cylinder head using inclined valves to

The Racing Mini

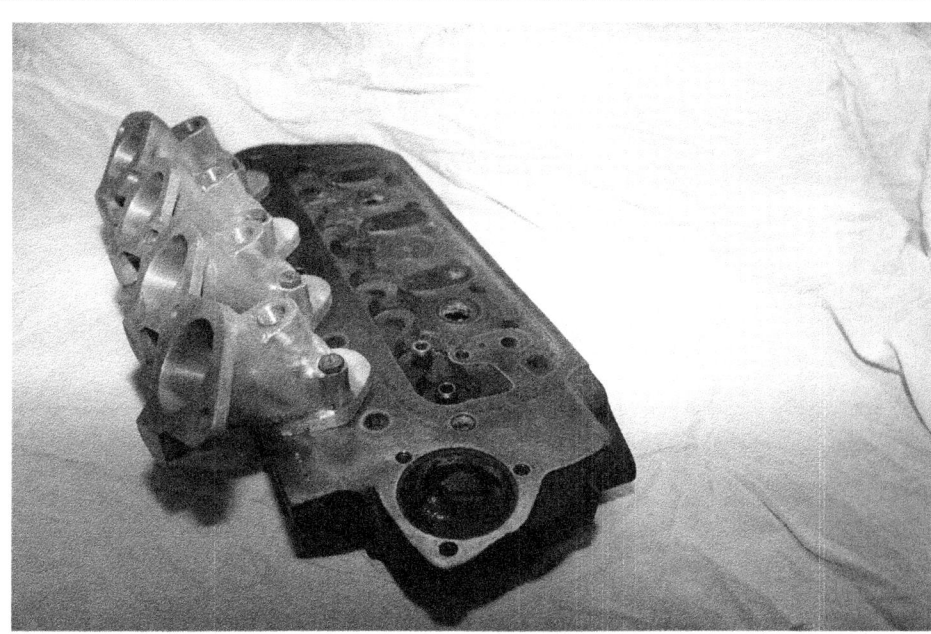

The cylinder head used on the fuel injected engine.

The special cam-shaft, with the extended nose to carry the pulley driving the metering unit.

allow for more breathing where the valve was adjacent to the wall of the combustion chamber. The inclined valve also had the effect of moving the point of contact of the valve stem further along the rocker thus giving very slight, but welcome, additional valve lift.

An 'eight port' or 'crossflow' cylinder head was also being developed by Weslake. The standard head with its three exhaust and two inlet ports all on one side of the engine was to be replaced with a more efficient set up of four inlets on the front side of the head and four exhausts on the back side. The promised arrival of the eight port head was a long time in being fulfilled and, much to the chagrin of John Cooper, a

The fuel injection metering unit.

71

Anatomy of the Works Minis

Accelerator cable acting on the rods to control the air and fuel supply.

private owner got his hands on one before he did.

Fuel injection

By 1967 the car was being raced under Group 5 regulations, which gave a lot more leeway regarding engine modifications. This allowed the use of the eight port head with fuel injection.

This was a Lucas system and was operated by a high-pressure pump beside the petrol tank, pumping fuel to a metering unit mounted in the position normally used by the alternator, which was repositioned to the bulkhead side of the engine. The metering unit was driven by a belt off the special camshaft, which was extended to protrude from the timing cover. As the barrel in the metering unit revolved it opened up ports feeding the appropriate cylinders. The fuel being fed in to the metering unit under high pressure forced a shuttle along a gallery which in turn forced the fuel through the port to the injector in the cylinder head. When the shuttle reached the end of its stroke, with its charge of fuel now behind it, the revolving barrel closed off the input port and opened one at the other end of the shuttle gallery forcing

The Racing Mini

the shuttle back and the fuel out of the next aligned port. The amount of fuel discharged was regulated by altering the length of the shuttle stroke. This was achieved by means of a rod acting on a stop in the metering unit, operated by the accelerator pedal. A second rod, operated by the same means, opened and closed a slide across the air intake. In this way the fuel to air ratio was synchronised.

Under Group 2 regulations cars up to 1000cc were only allowed to carry 60 litres and cars up to 1300cc 100 litres. An aluminium tank was made and fitted that complied with these regulations, but it had to be shaped to allow access to the spare wheel which, in 6-hour races, had to be used on the first pitstop.

This caused the centre of the tank to sit rather high. Under Group 5 regulations no spare wheel needed to be carried and this allowed for a rubber, foam filled tank to be fitted in the floor of the boot. This tank had a 'sump' that was lowered into the battery box to eliminate fuel surge and the fuel was picked up by the standard pump from this point and fed to the high pressure fuel injection pump.

The battery box was made deeper and a lightweight Varley battery, which could operate when dry, was slid on its side, into the false bottom.

The dry sump

Danny Richmond had also developed a 'dry sump' system. He had found some camshaft blanks with provision for a gear, extra to the one driving the distributor. Danny used this extra gear to drive an MGA oil pump mounted externally which was used to scavenge the oil from the engine back to an oil tank situated under the off-side front wing. The differential had a half inch of oil to keep it lubricated and the oil thrown by the crankshaft was sufficient to lubricate the gears. It had the desired effect of eliminating the constant problem of oil surge and gave an increase of power due to the crankshaft and con-rods not having to drag through the gallon of oil being churned up by the gearbox.

The flywheel was made of titanium, with a steel centre, and the face of the clutch release bearing was sprayed with sintered bronze to cut down the friction when the clutch was used. The clutch driven plate had a harder lining material and no cushioning springs. The starter ring was not secure when shrunk on to the titanium flywheel and had to be pinned into position.

This was the engine that was used by Gordon Spice when he lapped Silverstone at 1m 47.6secs. This was 1.4 seconds faster than Guiseppe Farina had lapped in the 4.5 litre formula one Ferrari some years previously. This computed to a lap speed of over 100mph!

The car with fuel injection was now producing 100bhp at the wheels when tested on the

Anatomy of the Works Minis

Abingdon rolling road. The best 'wet' sump engine fell four bhp short of this and the best Weber-carbed version gave 88-90 which was about 112bhp at the flywheel. The dry sump engine, although never tested on a dynamometer, was estimated to be giving around 122bhp at the flywheel.

The engine temperature increased in proportion to the extra power gained from it. The cooling system was improved, initially by using a modified radiator which had an extra row of waterways. This was augmented later by using the matrix out of a heater as a supplementary radiator, piped in to the heater water circuit. It was mounted by the side of the oil cooler. Later, the heater itself was used for additional cooling with the heat being fed from the demister ducts at the sides of the heater out through the floor of the car. It was also found that the old four-bladed fan was more efficient than the later multi-blade one that was fitted to reduce noise.

The limited-slip differential

Another innovation was the limited-slip differential. Two types were tried, the first of which was a friction type with the intervention of clutch plates between the output shafts. These plates could be adjusted to give between 40% to 100% drive to the inner wheel on cornering, when it had a tendency to lift off the road. The standard diff would take the line of least resistance and drive the wheel that was not in contact with the road, leaving the inner wheel, still on the road, with no drive!

The other system was the ZF diff. This was a cam and pawl design which locked progressively more as the power was fed to it. This system proved to be far too vicious on the front wheel drive cars as it tended to straighten the steering when power was applied (requiring extreme effort on the part of the driver to steer the car).

The clutch type was more acceptable, especially when set at 40%, although even this caused the car to behave erratically when driven on a light throttle under normal road conditions. This was to prove one of the drawbacks when fitted to the Works rally cars.

Tyres

The little ten inch Mini wheels revolving at high speed caused unacceptably high tyre temperatures, sometimes as much as 120 degrees C. These high temperatures arose through the flexing of the cords in the sidewalls of the tyres and forced the use of a harder compound rubber than that used by their competitors.

Ginger Devlin was the first to suggest the use of low profile tyres, to reduce the sidewall flexing, fitted to 12 inch wheels to keep the same rolling radius of the wheel/tyre assembly.

Dunlop accepted this suggestion and rapidly produced some low profile tyres to suit the larger diameter wheels with 6 inch and 8 inch widths. This

The Racing Mini

The new Mini on twelve inch wheels as pioneered by the Cooper Racing Team.

innovation was, in Ginger's words, "a winner", allowing as it did for the use of compounds two mixes softer. Temperatures were reduced to the 90s, and pressures, which had been high to limit 'wall flex', were reduced to 25lbs per sq. in.

The 12" wheel had little effect on the cars' initial speed while the tyres were comparatively cool, but after a couple of laps the advantage of the softer tyres and lower temperatures became obvious as the cars lapped at up to 2 seconds a lap faster. In addition to this, as the race progressed, the tyre on the ten inch wheel would have suffered from blistering and a tendency to throw its tread.

This was another mod that worked very well under track conditions but the low profile tyres, with very limited side wall flexibility, had an adverse effect on the car's handling properties when used under rally conditions. Paddy Hopkirk, during the 1969 Circuit of Ireland, attributed his 'off road excursions' to the new wheels. When back on the ten inch wheels, Paddy found the car much more to his liking.

Accessory modifications

The Group 5 regulations now allowed for all of the body panels to be made of aluminium. The only restriction being that the car should retain its original shape. A Microcell 'bucket' type driver's seat was fitted but the rest of the trim and seating had to remain as standard. The engine also had to remain in its original position.

Rapid gear changing could give rise to reverse being selected accidentally, so a 'gate' was fitted to stop this from happening. The driver could quickly release this gate if he had left the track, finishing up facing the wrong way and found that he needed to select reverse to get back on again.

Anatomy of the Works Minis

The value of a roll-over cage.

A roll cage was fitted and an extended steering rake bracket to lower the steering wheel. The instruments were on a panel in front of the driver and consisted of a rev counter, oil pressure and water temperature gauges. Also fitted was an old style Mini starter button to override the solenoid which was known to give trouble.

The starter bendix suffered the same as on the rally cars, in that clutch dust accumulated on the bendix and stopped it from engaging. The Cooper solution was to fit a length of $1/2$" pipe from the hole behind the starter to the radiator grill and, when required, a squirt of petrol got it working again.

Racing successes

The Mini's racing career started with Downton Engineering in 1959 and had tremendous success from 1961 when Sir John Whitmore won the British Saloon Car Championship in a Downton prepared Mini. The following year Whitmore and John Love were recruited by Cooper, and Love won the Championship. In 1963 the same pair contested the Championship and, again, Love was the more successful, coming second to Jack Sears who drove a Ford Galaxy.

In 1964 the Cooper racing team contested both the British and European Championships with Ken Tyrell looking after the European programme. This brought success for Warwick Banks who won the European Championship driving a 997cc car. 1965 saw the arrival, in the Cooper team, of John Rhodes who had started racing in Formula Junior in 1960. John took first place in the 1300cc Class in the British Championship and also won the 24-hour race at Spa. Meanwhile, his team-mate, Warwick Banks, was winning the 1000cc class and was second place overall in the Championship.

The Racing Mini

John Rhodes and Steve Neal battling at Druids, Brands Hatch.

In 1967 the BMC Competition Department entered a Mini in the 3-hour supporting race at the Sebring 12-hour Sports Car meeting. John Cooper was asked to prepare and provide a training car for the event. When it arrived in Abingdon it was checked over by the Abingdon mechanics who found that the brake pads and shoes were part worn. Doug Watts the Competition Department supervisor had an angry phone conversation with Ginger Devlin questioning the preparation of the car. Ginger apologised saying that brake pads and shoes on a racing Mini never wore out as most corners on a race track could be taken flat out in a Mini, with John Rhodes, in particular, who scrubbed off the speed by throwing the car sideways at a corner and entered it with the car pointing in the right direction for a quick exit.

The race car at Sebring was driven by John Rhodes and Paddy Hopkirk and won the 1300cc class.

Anatomy of the Works Minis

The BMC Works Racing Team at Cadwell Park 1969.

Later on that year BMC entered two 970cc Mini Cooper Ss in the 84-hour Marathon de La Route at Nurburgring. Tony Fall, Julien Vernaeve and Andrew Hedges were successful in their car, coming second overall to a Porsche 911. The second car, driven by Alec Poole, Clive Baker and the son of the MG Chief Designer, Roger Enever, retired following an accident.

The Works racers

In 1968 the BMC rallying was curtailed and the factory embarked upon a racing programme, but never achieved the same level of success as the specialist racing teams.

The racing programme threw up some interesting development projects for the Abingdon team. One of these was the further development of the eight port, or crossflow, cylinder head.

As with the Cooper engines, overheating was a major problem, and was the frequent cause of engine failure when partial seizure would collapse the top piston rings. The excessive heat would affect the cylinder head studs and gasket. This, combined with the high compression ratio, caused the head to lift allowing the water to escape into the cylinders and out of the engine altogether.

To combat this the BMC Mini racing engine was 'dry-decked'. This was a long and painstaking operation which involved doing away with the cylinder head gasket, having the faces of the head and block machined as flat as possible. Then, to achieve a perfect seal, the cylinder head was lapped onto the block by applying grinding paste to the surfaces and sliding the head back and forth across the block until an even grey colour on the faces indicated that the two were perfectly mated.

The waterways between the head and block were sealed off so that if the head were to lift there would be a loss of power but no loss of water to cause terminal damage to the engine. A pipe was fitted into the water jacket of the block and a hose carried the water to an auxiliary radiator mounted at the front of the car next to the oil cooler and from there back to the cylinder head. It was found, however, that steam would build up in the top of the head, so a small pipe was inserted to allow this steam to escape and feed back into the system.

Appendix B
The Rallycross Mini
(Based on information supplied by 'Jumping Jeff' Williamson)

Joining the Works team

In 1969 the Competitions Department turned its attention to the sport of Rallycross which brought to light a whole new set of specialist drivers. One of these was Jeff Williamson, whose driving technique earned him the soubriquet 'Jumping Jeff' because of his ability to take off from a crest and jump farther and higher than his competitors. Another was Brian Chatfield. These two were recruited from the ranks of the Mini drivers who were making a name for themselves in rallycross, the sport made popular by regular showing on

Jeff Williamson with his first Works car at Lydden Hill in 1970.

The Rallycross Mini

John Rhodes, Jeff Williamson and Brian Chatfield chasing Rod Chapman's Ford Escort.

Saturday afternoon television. They joined the racing drivers John Rhodes and John Handley to form the British Leyland Racing Team.

Four cars were prepared for the team, each with a different specification. John Rhodes' car was on 'dry' suspension, with an eight port head and fuel injection. John Handley had hydrolastic suspension and carburettors. Jeff and Brian had cars with five port heads and split Webers, Brian's car had hydrolastic suspension, whilst Jeff's had dry suspension. The drivers were not consulted on the specifications of their cars, but Jeff recalls that he didn't mind that: he had a Works drive and he was to be paid for doing something he enjoyed, albeit earning only £10 a day plus expenses!

Previously, Jeff had prepared and raced his own Minis with considerable success, he won an invitation race in his Riley Elf and, at the same meeting, qualified for the final of a knockout competition against John Rhodes who had a one-off Works 1300 powered by an eight port fuel injected engine. Jeff's car had worn itself out winning the main event so Peter Browning loaned him John Handley's similarly engined car. However, despite leading for much of the race he was narrowly beaten by the more experienced John Rhodes. It was after this event that he was offered the Works drive.

The team cars showed their Works rallying heritage with padding where knees and elbows came in contact with the car's bodywork. The John Aley roll cage was a simple loop across the car with a bar going from the centre to the reinforced rear parcel shelf. The 'T' shackle that joined the bars was covered with

81

Anatomy of the Works Minis

The Rallycross Mini

Second place in the snow at Croft in 1970.

a tailor-made padded leather sheath from the factory Trim Department which clipped into place with press-studs. The driver's seat was fibreglass

Opposite top: Jumping Jeff in his Riley Elf.

Opposite bottom: Jeff Williamson winning the BBC TV Rallycross at Lydden Hill, having given up the struggle to keep the windscreen clear, he removed it!

mounted into a steel frame and bolted to the floor. The body panels were especially pressed aluminium expertly fitted and indistinguishable from the original. Jeff was greatly impressed with such refinements comparing his own shoestring efforts of ill-fitting fibreglass panels pop riveted on to the stripped door frames. Rallycrossing was a tough sport and the private owner couldn't

afford to replace expensive panels after every race. However, the Works cars, being the focus of the television cameras, had to look pristine under all conditions on the start line.

The interior, however, was a different matter and the Works cars were just as spartan inside as the non-Works. They were stripped of all non-essentials, including the passenger seat,

Anatomy of the Works Minis

Mini Rallycross engine with Amal Carburettors on the crossflow cylinder head.

carpets, etc. The dash panel held the oil pressure/water temperature gauge, the ignition switch, the fuel pump switch and the rev counter. The latter's capacity of reading up to 10,000rpm was, perhaps, a bit optimistic, although engine speeds in excess of 7000rpm could be expected. Mounted below the dash were the battery cut-out switch and the starter button. There were no lights fitted, so minimal wiring was needed. The double fuel pump was mounted under the rear seat on the passenger's side, and fuel and battery lines were run through the inside of the car.

The split Webers on Jeff's car were mounted onto a special steel manifold. The stringent rallying regulations called for the carburettors to be mounted on the standard manifolds, which meant that the normal mounting flange on the Weber carb had to be cut off and replaced by an SU type flange. As the material of these items was cast aluminium, welding them together was a difficult and not always successful job. The more relaxed rallycross rules allowed for the flanges to be left alone and the manifold to be changed.

Life after Comps closed
The Competition Department was closed in 1970 and a much curtailed competition pro-gramme, including support for the Minis in rallycross, was carried on by the Special Tuning Department under the management of Basil Wales. Jeff Williamson was one of the more prominent competitors in the televised sport and he was given the car that he had rallycrossed with so much success. When the Mini became Jeff's own property he took a greater interest in its history and realised that it was originally a Mk1 bodyshell that

The Rallycross Mini

had been made to look like a Mk2. It was painted the traditional red with a white roof.

Further enquiries led him to believe that the car had previously seen action as John Handley's entry on the Tour-de-France in 1969 carrying the registration No. URX 560G. The more that Jeff found out about his car, the more he was impressed with the attention to detail that could only have been the result of having almost unlimited time and money spent on it. He was also impressed with the 'dry-decked' engine which was more evidence of its racing heritage.

A further refinement was the adjustable rear break limiter valve. This valve allows only a set pressure to reach the rear brakes because the light rear end of the Mini doesn't need as much stopping power as the front. The brake pressure acts on a valve with a spring behind it; when the pre-determined pressure is reached the spring is compressed sufficiently to close the valve and stop any further pressure reaching the brake shoes. There are different grades of limiter valves to be used on the various Mini derivatives, these are governed by the strength of the spring. The valve is normally fitted on the rear subframe, but the Works drivers found that on rallies that ran over various surfaces, such as, where a stage on a loose surface is followed by a speed test on a race track, the balance of the brakes needed to be adaptable. A system was developed whereby the spring tension could be adjusted by an external screw. These valves were brought inside the car where they were readily accessible to the crew. Jeff's car was so equipped, although, on a short event such as a rallycross he never found the need to adjust it once he had found an acceptable setting.

The quest for more power
In an attempt to get more power, a Westlake prepared iron crossflow head was tried with two 45 DCOE Weber carburettors. This in its turn was replaced by an Arden aluminium crossflow head with four Amal carbs. The cubic capacity of the engine was greatly increased, sometimes to as much as 1500cc. This was achieved by using the MG 1300 cylinder block bored out to +.120 and using Triumph pistons. This called for the bores to be offset and a lot of cylinder blocks were ruined before a good one was produced. A long throw crankshaft made out of a solid billet of special steel was another costly but effective method of gaining the valuable increase in engine capacity.

One engine that Jeff acquired was a fuel injected turbocharged 1293 unit that gave an enormous 180bhp. This was in a car that had been used in circuit racing by Alec Poole but it proved to be not so effective on rallycross and Jeff later sold it to a customer in Jamaica.

Such was the competition that some of Jeff's competitors

Anatomy of the Works Minis

went to even greater lengths. The engines on some Minis were replaced altogether with the powerful Ford 16 valve BDA engines grafted onto the Mini gearbox!

Suspension mods

In the free and easy world of rallycross almost anything was allowed, and over the years Jeff tried many variations of suspension set-ups. The first was an independent set-up of his own devising. The back half of the rear subframe was cut off, but the radius arms were retained, still swivelling on the brackets on the front half of the frame. The rubber springs were discarded as were the standard shock absorbers. These items were replaced by a shock absorber inside an adjustable spring. Jeff admits that it was a bit crude but saved a considerable amount of weight, and the adjustable springs were of great benefit.

Another method entailed doing away with the rear subframe entirely and replacing it with a simple beam axle located by four forward facing parallel links and again using the adjustable coil spring over shock absorber system. However, although this was successful and widely used by the circuit racers, the beam axle proved not to give any advantage on rallycross.

Twelve inch wheels were sometimes used on the front of the car and, according to the profile of the tyres, this would involve changing the ride height. An ingenious method of carrying this out was devised by a friend of Jeffs, Tony Chemmings, who asked Jeff to do initial testing on the system

The High-Lo system for adjusting the Mini ride height.

The Rallycross Mini

Four-wheel-drive Mini with modified rear suspension and drive to rear wheels.

called the High-Lo system. It was fairly straightforward, the trumpet acting on the rubber spring was threaded and adjusted through the top of the subframe with a 'T' bar. The system was refined and marketed with great success.

Four-wheel-drive

Although I have previously described the four-wheel-drive Mini in my earlier book *Works Rally Mechanic* I make no apology for doing so again as I feel that no account of rallycross is complete without it.

Minis were taking centre-stage on Saturday afternoon television, being ideally suited to the sport (much to the chagrin of their great rivals, Ford).

This was a situation that the Ford hierarchy could not allow to continue, so a V6 Capri was modified to take the four-wheel-drive system that had been previously used on the Ferguson PP9, the only four-wheel-drive car to win a Formula One race. What was more, Ford's most successful driver, Roger Clark, was in the driving seat. Needless to say it stole the Mini's thunder, causing a reaction from the Leyland hierarchy in its turn.

Basil Wales, the boss of the Abingdon-based Special Tuning Department was instructed to "Do something about it." The "something" was a second look at a vehicle currently being used to tow 'non-runners' off

Anatomy of the Works Minis

Hugh Wheldon in the four-wheel-drive Mini.

the production lines. This was an 'Ant,' a derivation of the Moke which was equipped with the desired four-wheel-drive. The now defunct Competition Department had looked at the possibility of using this system but there was little motivation at the time.

The gearbox, modified as it was to accommodate the extra pinion on the differential, was from an 850 Mini, and the central web of the gearbox had to be machined to take the longer throw of the 1275 crankshaft. The drive from the extra pinion was carried via a propshaft to another diff mounted at the rear of the car. From here the drive was taken to the wheels by Cooper 'S' driveshafts. The rear subframe was discarded and special radius arms, with provision for the driveshaft and hub assembly, were mounted on brackets in what would be the front fixing points of the subframe to the body. The rubber Mini suspension springs were pierced with 6 large holes to weaken them and soften the suspension. These operated vertically between the radius arm and a plate in the boot floor.

The 'knife and fork' modification had several drawbacks, one was the absence of a differential between the front

The Rallycross Mini

Jumping Jeff still campaigning the ex-works Mini in the 1990s.

and rear wheels. This was not a big problem in the wet when the wheels could spin to keep in synchronisation but it made the car a handful in the dry.

Another drawback was the gearchange. Because of the position of the propshaft, the gearchange rod came out of the top of the diff casing and through the front bulkhead to a bracket mounted on the propshaft tunnel and finished up operating the opposite way to normal *i.e.* 1st where 4th should be and *vice versa*. Additionally, the tunnel mounting could not be made to compensate for the torque movement of the engine and the rod snapped. The diagnosis of the cause of this fault was not made before it had failed twice on one event and was welded between races.

The whole assembly, mated to a 1293cc eight-port headed engine with four Amal carburettors, was built into a Mini Clubman.

My earlier information was that the first driver was Hugh Wheldon but Jeff maintains that Brian Chatfield was the first driver of the FWD Mini on its debut race at Lydden Hill. No announcement had been made and it was not until Brian was seen taking a corner flat out on opposite lock with all wheels spinning that the paddock crowd realised that this was something different. The first race started with the Mini leaping away from the start leaving the FWD Ford in its wake. Alas, however, the diff that had toiled away for several years in the factory was

89

Anatomy of the Works Minis

Steering column gear change mechanism. Note the rev counter warning at 8000rpm.

not up to the task and gave up before the end of the race, but not before being the focus of attention for the TV cameras. This was towards the end of the season and the car was not used again until the start of the 1971 season. The diff had failed before the gear selection rod problem had reared its head and so had not been rectified in the interim.

Hugh Wheldon drove it in the first race of the 1971 season, again at Lydden Hill, in front of the BBC cameras. Jeff was scheduled to drive it the following week at Cadwell Park in an event covered by ITV. Again the Mini's race came to an end before the gear change broke, this time through a collision with a FWD BDA-engined Daf, which caused the Mini to roll, and Jeff was told not to expect the car to be repaired by the next weekend. However, some burning of Special Tuning midnight oil saw the car, complete with a new roof, ready by the following Thursday.

Jeff was leading the field toward the end of the first heat when the gear rod gave way. It was stripped out and welded for the next heat, (which, incidentally, ITV held up until we were ready, such was the interest in the car). Again the car was proving a winner when the rod snapped again.

The Rallycross Mini

Back at the factory some high-tech designing with a piece of chalk on the workshop floor brought forth a solution. Run the rod via a Triumph steering column flexible joint and a couple of rose joints, to a gear lever behind the steering wheel. Jeff never drove the car again but it went on to win many races before being overpowered by the monster-engined Dafs, Fords, and VW-lookalike Porsches.

Jeff's original ex-Works Mini suffered a total write-off, rolling end over end while competing in a BTRDA Autocross at Weeford Park near Sutton Coldfield. The bits were rebuilt to Group 1 spec, however, into another ex-Abingdon shell. He used this car to compete in a number of rallies in the seventies including the Manx and the Tour of Britain.

In the eighties Jeff only competed in two events, the RAC Golden Fifty in 1982 and the Coronation Rally in 1983.

The car was unused from that time until 1996, when Jeff dug it out to do the Deutschland Rally, and again in 1997 for the Hunsruck Rally. Since then there has been a Players No. 6 Autocross (at Thorseby), a rallycross at Lydden Hill and the 40th Birthday Rallysprint at Silverstone in 1999. The engine has remained virtually untouched since 1976 and the body, bearing the scars of Jeff's aggressive driving technique, was due for replacement. In time it will be returned to its former glory with Jeff continuing with his philosophy of "Use 'em and abuse 'em. That's what they were made for."

OTHER RELATED BOOKS FROM VELOCE -

Paperback, 160 pages, over 150 colour and b&w pictures
ISBN: 978-1-904788-18-8/UPC: 6-36847-00318-0
Brian Moylan spent 22 years preparing cars for international rallies and travelling the world to provide service support. A hugely entertaining story of adventure, hardship, winning, losing and real danger.

Paperback, 128 pages, 350 colour & b&w photographs,
ISBN: 978-1-787111-67-7/UPC:6-36847-01167-3
An invaluable guide for the home restorer. Coverage includes: tools; panel removal/fitting; sectional repairs; sills, floors and outriggers; chassis members; multiple panel assemblies; metal forming techniques; tricks of the trade, and much, much more.

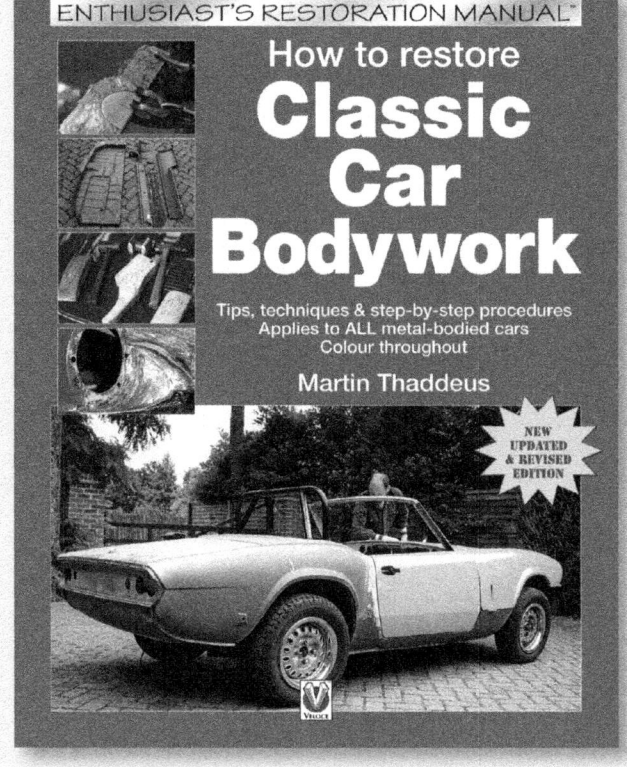

*P&P extra. Prices subject to change.
For details visit www.veloce.co.uk or call 01305 260068.

Paperback, 144 pages, over 150 colour & b&w pictures
ISBN: 978-1-845848-69-9/UPC: 6-36847-04869-3
A complete guide to obtaining maxmum power, with reliability, from this classic engine that saw use in many Mini models.

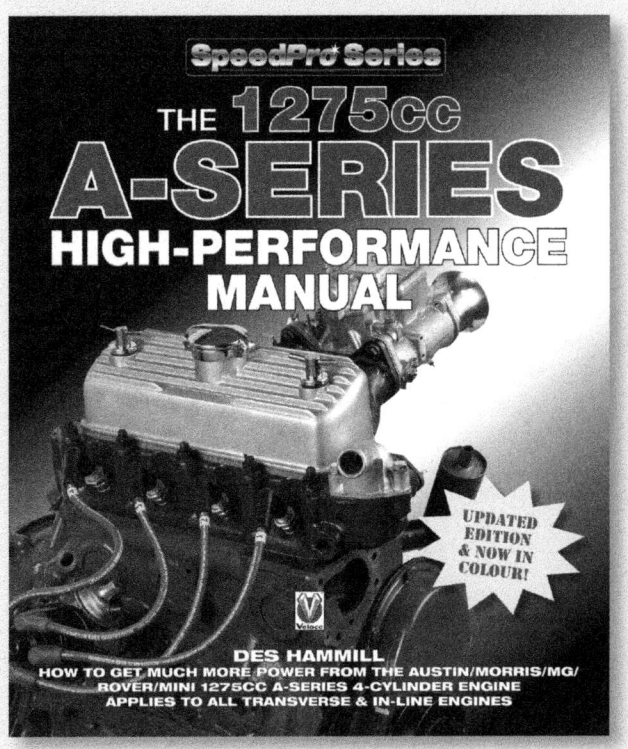

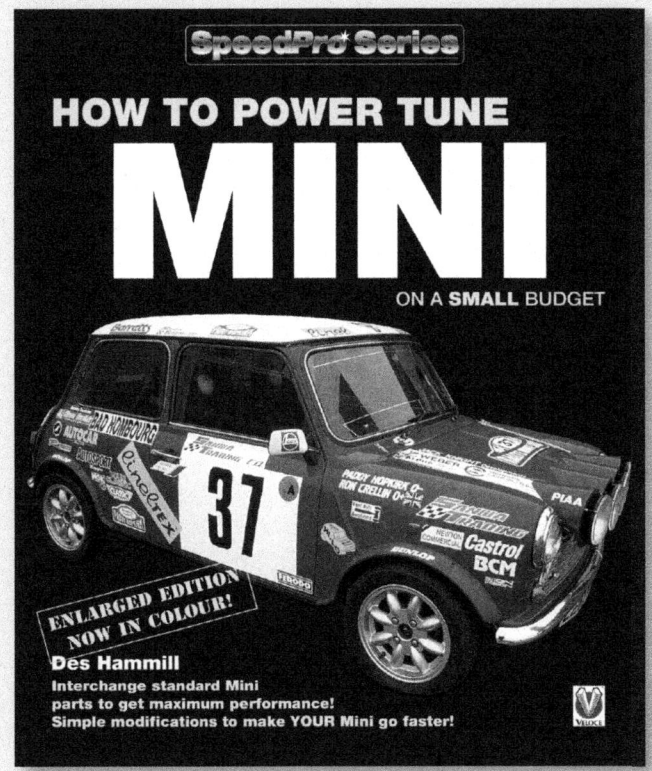

Paperback, 104 pages, over 50 colour & b&w pictures
ISBN: 978-1-787110-87-8/UPC: 6-36847-01087-4
This book reveals the secrets of how to use alternative 'bolt-on' parts (readily available from Austin-Rover dealers, scrapyards and automotive supply outlets) to improve Mini engine performance.

*P&P extra. Prices subject to change.
For details visit www.veloce.co.uk or call
01305 260068.

Index

Illustrations in **bold**.

Aaltonen, Raunno 36, 49, 56, **57**
Abingdon 7
Accelerator pedal modification **35**
Aley, John 81
Alpine Rally 1963 37
Amal carburettors **84**
Asbestos 29
Austin Healey 7
Autocross 91

Baker, Clive 78
Banks, Warwick 76, 77
Baxter, Raymond 47
BMC 9
BMC Works Racing team **78**
BMIHT Gaydon 6
Bradford, Stan 24, 55
Bramley, Tony 9
Broad, Ralph 69
Browning, Peter 6, 81
BTRDA 91
Build sheet **10, 11, 12, 13, 14, 15, 16**
Burnell, Eddie 65
Burnt-out Mini, 1962 Monte **57**
  Under bonnet **58**
  Interior **58**

Carter, Mick 28, 43
Cave, Willy 37
Centre-lock Mini wheel assembly **40**
  In situ **40**
  Spanners **41**
Challis, Neville 9, 45
Chalmers, Stan 22
Chambers, Marcus 6, 7
Chapman, Rod **81**
Chatfield, Brian 80, **81**, 89
Chemmings, Tony 87
Clark, Roger 87
Con-rod balancing **44**
Cookson 28
Cooper, John 6, 67, 70, 77
Coronation Rally 91
Crusader tanks 9

DAF 90, 91
Delamont, Dean 69
Denton, Bill 28
Deutschland Rally 91
Devlin, Ginger 6, 69, 74, 77
'Dog House' 24
Downton 29, 62, 70, 76
Druids, Brands Hatch **77**
Dunlop 75

Easter, Paul **22**

Anatomy of the Works Minis

Electric defrosters **20**
Enever, Roger **78**
Engine mounting rubber **61**
Engine steady bar **60**

Fall, Tony 6, 43, **52**, 78
Farina, Guiseppe **73**
Ferguson PP9 **87**
Ferrari **73**
'Fly-off' handbrake modification **35**
Ford Capri **87**
Ford Escort **81**
Ford Galaxy **76**
Four-wheel-drive gear change **90**
Four-wheel drive Mini **88**
Four-wheel drive suspension **87**
Frilford golf course **24**

German Rally 1966 6, **43**
Grainger, Rod **6**
Green, Den 6, **10**

Halda Speedpilot **24**
Halda Twinmaster **25**
Handley, John 41, 81, **85**
Headlamp flasher switch **54**
Hedges, Andrew **78**
Heuer clocks **26**
Hi-Lo adjustable suspension **86**
Hopkirk, Paddy 20, **64**, 75, 78
Humphreys, Cliff 6, **46**, **64**, 70
Hunts of Poole **45**

Interior painted matt black **23**

Liddon, Henry 6, **49**
Lightening holes **18**
Love, John **76**
Lucas 22, **53**, 72
Lydden Hill **91**

Mackinen, Timo **21**

Maher, Eddie **70**
Manx Rally **91**
MG factory yard **8**
MGA chassis assembly **29**
MGB **28**
Mini on 1970 World Cup **39**
Minis in the workshop **8**
 Repainted in red & white **18**
Mintex **48**
Mitchell, Terry 62, 6,
Modified front shocker mounting bracket **31**
Monte Carlo Rally 1967 **39**
Monte Carlo Rally 1968 **55**
Monte Carlo winner 1965 9, **47**

Navigational aids **22**
Nurburgring **78**

Petrol tank strap **56**
Petrol tank strap modification **57**
Poole, Alec **85**
Porsche **78**
Press Shop **28**
Price, Bill **6**
Proctor, Stuart **69**

Quick lift jack brackets **26**
Quick lift jack in action **27**

RAC Golden 50 **91**
RAC Rally 1959 **7**
Rallycross, with no windscreen **82**
Rhodes, John 76, 77, 78, **81**
Richmond, Danny **73**
Riley **28**
Roll-over cage **76**

Scott, Jack **20**
Seal, Tom **6**
Sears, Jack **76**
Seat brackets **17**
Sebring **78**

Shell 4000 in Canada **27**
Sibbald, Michael **6**
Silverstone **91**
Smith, John 22, **53**
Speedo drive off rear wheel **28**
Spice, Gordon **73**
Sprinzel, John **37**
Steering column accident **37**
Stevens, Dick **28**
Straight-cut gears **50**

Taylor, Henry **69**
Thornley, John **7**
Tie-bar protection **31**
Tour de Corsica **48**
Tour de France 1969 **41**
Tour de France knock-on wheels **42**
Tour of Britain **91**
Triumph **91**
Turner, Stuart 6, **69**
Tyrell, Ken **76**

Vale of White Horse District Council **25**
Vernaeve, Julien **78**

Wales, Basil 6, 84, 87,
Watts, Doug 10, **77**
Weber carburettors **7**
Wellman, Tommy 6, **10**
Wheldon, Hugh **88**, 89, 90
Whitmore, John (Sir) **76**
Whittington, Bob **44**
Williamson, Jeff 6, **80**, **81**, **82**, **83**, **84**, **89**, 90, 91,
Windscreen washer bottle **19**

95

Anatomy of the Works Minis

Printed and bound by CPI Group (UK) Ltd, Croydon, CR0 4YY
22/03/2026
02076210-0001